Reading to
Understand
Science

McGraw-Hill Basic Skills System

Tools for Learning Success

Tests

STUDY SKILLS	READING	VOCABULARY	SPELLING	WRITING	MATH
Study Skills	Efficient Rates	Vocabulary Skills	Spelling Skills	Writing Skills 1	Arithmetic
Problem Solving	The Main Idea		Basic Spelling	Writing Skills 2	Elementary Algebra
Listening & Notetaking	Significant Facts			Paragraph Patterns	Intermediate Algebra
Underlining	Organization				
Library & Reference Skills	Main Idea in Science				
	Critical Reading				
	Study-Type Reading				
	Skimming and Scanning				

Materials

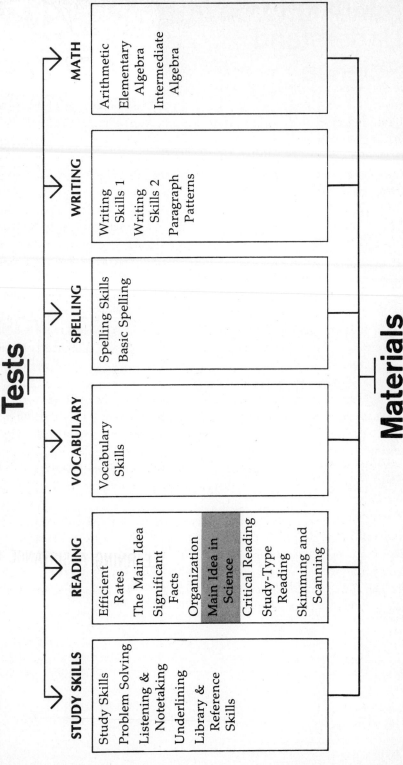

Editor's Introduction

This book is one of eight parts in a series devoted to instruction in reading skills. This reading series, in turn, is part of a larger system of instructional materials—the McGraw-Hill Basic Skills System: Tools for Learning Success. Designed at the University of Minnesota Reading and Study Skills Center, the Basic Skills System is aimed at college-bound high school students, and junior college and college students who need to improve those skills necessary for academic success. The system consists of *tests* to determine instructional needs and *materials* designed to meet those needs, plus an instructor's manual to explain the tests and materials and the relationship between them. The purpose of the *tests* is to find out what instruction a student needs in basic skills, and the purpose of the *materials* is to give him that instruction. Each student gets what he needs without wasting time on unnecessary tasks.

Six basic skill topics—study, reading, vocabulary, spelling, writing, and mathematics—are covered, and two tests (A and B forms) are provided for each topic. Subscales on the tests are matched to accompanying instructional materials: thus a student with a low score on one or more subscales gets instruction in the corresponding skill. The second form of the test may be used to evaluate progress after instruction.

The materials in the Basic Skills System have been field-tested and revised to provide the best possible results. While most of the materials are self-instructional programs, the tests, of course, are designed for supervised administration. These testing instruments have been carefully developed and standardized by California Test Bureau. The latest research techniques and procedures have been utilized to ensure the highest possible validity and reliability.

The instructional materials are designed to be used separately, if desired, and can be purchased as single units. Most of the materials are suitable for adoption as textbooks in such basic skill courses as Freshman English, Communications, How to Study, Vocabulary Development, and Remedial or Developmental Mathematics. Individualized diagnosis and instruction are optional in such settings.

Alton L. Raygor
Consulting Editor
University of Minnesota

Reading to Understand Science

A Program for
Self-instruction

JOSEPH A. FISHER
Associate Professor of Education
Director, Reading and Study Skills Clinic
Drake University

McGRAW-HILL BOOK COMPANY
New York   St. Louis   San Francisco   Düsseldorf
London   Mexico   Panama   Sydney   Toronto

07-051382-1

34567890 DODO 79876

McGraw-Hill Basic Skills System:
Design Director: Barbara Bert
Production Supervisor: Adam Jacobs
Editing Supervisor: Albert Shapiro
Editor: James Wallace
Manuscript Development: Alice Hopkins

Acknowledgments
for the Readings

Acknowledgment is made for the use of materials from the following sources.

Baker, Robert H., *Astronomy,* 8th ed., D. Van Nostrand Company, Inc., Princeton, N. J., 1964, pp. 63–64 (pp. 96, 98 of this book)

Bierstedt, Robert, *The Social Order,* 2d ed., McGraw-Hill Book Company, New York, 1957, pp. 157–158 (pp. 132, 134 of this book), p. 380 (p. 64 of this book)

Branson, E. B., W. A. Tarr, and W. D. Keller, *Introduction to Geology,* 3d ed., McGraw-Hill Book Company, New York, 1952, p. 157 (p. 16 of this book), pp. 362–363 (pp. 24, 104, 106 of this book), p. 239 (p. 138 of this book)

DeCoursey, Russel Myles, *The Human Organism,* 3d ed., McGraw-Hill Book Company, 1968, p. 515 (pp. 88, 90 of this book), pp. 22–23 (p. 52 of this book)

Freeman, Otis W., and H. F. Raup, *Essentials of Geography,* 2d ed., McGraw-Hill Book Company, 1959, p. 56 (pp. 180, 182 of this book), p. 270 (p. 190 of this book)

Hailstones, T. J., and J. H. Dodd, *Economics—An Analysis of Principles and Policies,* 5th ed., Southwestern Publishing Company, Dallas, 1965, p. 484 (pp. 164, 166 of this book), p. 356 (p. 168 of this book), p. 353 (pp. 172, 174 of this book)

Krauskopf, Konrad, and Arthur Beiser, *The Physical Universe,* McGraw-Hill Book Company, New York, 1960, p. 69 (pp. 30, 32 of this book), p. 122 (pp. 140, 142 of this book); pp. 152–153 (pp. 144, 146 of this book), p. 56 (p. 186 of this book)

McConnell, Campbell R., *Economics—Principles, Problems, and Policies,* 3d ed., McGraw-Hill Book Company, 1966, p. 672 (pp. 124, 126 of this book), p. 60 (p. 74 of this book), p. 52 (pp. 192, 194 of this book)

Moore, J. A. (sup.), *Biological Science, An Inquiry into Life,* Harcourt, Brace, & World, Inc., New York, 1963, p. 95 (p. 38 of this book), p. 689 (p. 56 of this book)

Morgan, Clifford T., and Richard A. King, *Introduction to Psychology,* 3d ed., McGraw-Hill Book Company, 1966, pp. 76–77 (pp. 128, 130 of this book), p. 489 (p. 62 of this book), p. 192 (pp. 70, 72 of this book), p. 531 (p. 162 of this book), p. 123 (p. 160 of this book), p. 253 (pp. 176, 178 of this book), p. 287 (p. 188 of this book)

Petrovich, M. B., and P. D. Curtin, *The Human Achievement,* Silver Burdett Company, Morristown, N. J., 1967, p. 175 (p. 60 of this book), p. 57 (pp. 66, 68 of this book), p. 177 (pp. 76, 78 of this book), p. 540 (p. 84 of this book), p. 495 (pp. 80, 82 of this book)

Sartain, Aaron Quinn, Alvin John North, Jack Roy Strange, and Harold Martin Chapman, *Psychology: Understanding Human Behavior,* McGraw-Hill Book Company, New York, 3d ed., 1967, pp. 40–41, (pp. 100, 102 of this book), p. 241 (p. 116 of this book)

Slurzberg, Morris, and William Osterheld, *Essentials of Electricity-Electronics,* 3d ed., McGraw-Hill Book Company, New York, 1965, p. 147 (p. 10 of this book)

Smith, Alpheus W., and John N. Cooper, *Elements of Physics,* 7th ed., McGraw-Hill Book Company, 1964, pp. 146–147 (p. 4 of this book), pp. 82–83 (pp. 18, 112 of this book), pp. 44–45 (pp. 34, 36 of this book), p. 146 (p. 152 of this book), p. 150 (p. 154 of this book)

Storer, Tracy I., Robert L. Usinger, and James W. Nybakken, *Elements of Zoology,* 3d ed., McGraw-Hill Book Company, New York, 1968, p. 4 (p. 204 of this book), p. 78 (pp. 92, 94 of this book), p. 235 (p. 114 of this book)

Weisz, Paul B., *Elements of Biology,* McGraw-Hill Book Company, 2d ed., 1965, p. 20 (p. 120 of this book)

—— , *Elements of Biology,* 3d ed., McGraw-Hill Book Company, 1969, p. 41 (p. 198 of this book), p. 56 (p. 200 of this book), pp. 6–7 (p. 202 of this book), p. 3 (p. 206 of this book), p. 5 (p. 208 of this book), p. 11 (p. 118 of this book)

—— , *Laboratory Manual for the Science of Zoology,* McGraw-Hill Book Company, New York, 1967, p. 68 (pp. 148, 150 of this book)

—— and Melvin S. Fuller, *The Science of Botany,* McGraw-Hill Book Company, New York, 1962, p. 44 (pp. 40, 108, 110 of this book), p. 43 (pp. 42, 44 of this book), p. 50 (pp. 46, 48, 50 of this book), pp. 85–86 (p. 54 of this book)

For

Lawrence Lutze
Bazil Stegman
Malacky Sullivan
William Eller

Teachers who have made a difference
in my life and the lives of many
others.

Preface

Because of its increased importance in our daily lives, science has been given considerable emphasis in today's educational program. Skills in reading scientific material, therefore, have become proportionately more important for students who wish to succeed in today's curriculum. But reading is a complex process, and not all the important and necessary basic skills are learned equally well by every individual. It is possible to progress through secondary school and still have certain handicaps in reading which make us less efficient students than we could be.

Education has long recognized that the kind of reading skills required in the fields of science are different from those needed in other fields, such as literature, for example; but to date not many special materials have been developed to improve specifically science reading skills. "Reading to Understand Science" is an effort to remedy this situation. In it the student is given help in analyzing and practicing the more important abilities demanded for efficient reading in various fields of science. The purpose of this text is:

1. To provide a series of reading exercises which develop skills necessary for effective reading in the various fields of science.
2. To provide students with insight into the kinds of thinking involved in scientific writing.
3. To direct students through a series of well-constructed exercises which will prepare them to transfer their new skills to the reading skills needed in any particular field of scientific study.

This book is part of a series offering a comprehensive program in reading improvement. Therefore, the present volume is able to concentrate on developing only those skills which have special application to the reading of science. It is assumed that students needing help in other related reading skills will turn to other books in the series. When necessary, these other texts may be studied together with the present volume.

"Reading to Understand Science" is divided into five principle parts. Part 1 deals with understanding principal ideas in material that is read. This portion of the manual consists of a number of selections from current texts in the physical sciences and social sciences, each followed by a series of questions designed to help the student think through and identify the principal idea of the selection.

To completely understand and retain the principal idea of a selection, it is necessary to understand how supporting ideas are related to it. In Part 2, the student is given practice in understanding supporting ideas. In this section, which also consists of reading selections taken from various science texts, he learns how to recognize definitions given in context and the use and function of explanation, illustration, and comparison as the rhetorical means for clarifying ideas. Because in much writing these various techniques are found in combinations, several selections are included in which a number of these techniques occur simultaneously.

Part 3 is called Understanding Experiments. The ability to observe, record accurately, and follow instructions are essential skills in learning and understanding science. By learning to look for the purpose of experiments or directions, and becoming aware of the importance of sequence, the student can develop his powers of observation and sense of order, both of which are required for efficient laboratory skills.

Part 4 is called Understanding Graphic Aids. In this unit the student is given practical suggestions on how to gain meaning from graphs, charts, diagrams, and tables. Since these aids are used to emphasize or clarify ideas discussed in the science text, understanding these aids is an important learning skill for students of science.

The selections in Part 5, Understanding Scientific Principles, present general concepts of science. Using the science reading skills already developed, the student is asked to summarize the essential meaning of passages from science textbooks.

"Reading to Understand Science" is written and arranged for self-instruction so that any student may work to improve his science reading skills on his own. The content is also adaptable for use in classroom instruction; in courses in developmental reading it can serve as a complete self-contained unit of instruction. It is a useful adjunct to a study skills program since reading science is frequently an area of study problems. However it is used, the student benefits because he must face and solve problems rather than read and remember answers. His active involvement develops understanding and makes transfer of skills much more likely.

Joseph A. Fisher

Acknowledgments

The author owes a debt of gratitude to many persons who have helped make this book possible. Among those the author would like to acknowledge with a special word of thanks are the students in the Reading and Study Skills Clinic at Drake University; Professor Robert J. Vanden Branden of the Science Education Department of Drake University for his counsel and helpful suggestions when they were needed most; Mrs. Margaret Foglesong, without whose patience and diligence there would have been no manuscript at all; and my dear wife and children for the patience, understanding, and sacrifice which dad's writing demands of them.

Joseph A. Fisher

To the Student

The exercises in this book differ from most written teaching materials in that they are *programmed:* that is, information is presented in small segments, called frames, which ask you to answer a question before going on to the next segment. By responding to these questions, you share in the development of the material you are studying. You are constantly made aware of your learning progress because the questions are always answered before you begin the next frame. If you cannot answer a given question, you should review the preceding frames and try again. The material has been prepared so that you will make very few mistakes if you read the material carefully.

You will be asked to read passages taken from textbooks in the physical and social sciences. Then you will do the accompanying exercises for each passage. The exercises will help you become more aware of the structure of the paragraphs, of the main points the author is making, and of the way he supports his main ideas. The sections on Experiments and Graphic Aids should be especially helpful to you in your future reading of scientific texts.

You will be asked to make three kinds of responses to the material in this book. Sometimes the questions can be answered with one word or number or letter, sometimes with more than one word, and sometimes more extensive responses are required.

To enable you to see at a glance which kind of response is expected of you, three different methods are used:

1. A single blank line within the sentence means that the answer is one word (or number or letter).
2. A double set of lines means that the answer is two or more words.
3. Single blank lines extending across the whole column mean that a more extensive answer is required.

Below are some examples of how you will respond to the exercises in the book. The directions may ask you to:

1. Supply a missing word or words. For example:
   Each frame requires one of several types of _____.

Answer: response.

2. Select a term from several provided to complete a statement. For example:
The reader should (respond, not respond) _____
to the question in each frame.

    a. Respond.

    b. Not respond.

Answer: *a.*

3. Match a term with a statement. For example:

a.	Single blank line	1. _____	Answer is two or more words.
b.	Double set of lines	2. _____	More extensive answer is required.
c.	Single blank lines extending across the page	3. _____	Answer is one word (or number or letter).

Answer: *b, c, a.*

Briefly, these are the procedures to follow in using this text:

1. Read the selection presented on the left-hand page.
2. Read the exercises on the right-hand page.
3. Write your response to each frame in the space provided.
4. Check your answer by comparing it with the correct response given below each question. In some cases you may not have exactly the same words as the response. As long as the answer you have given has the same meaning, you may consider your response correct.
5. If your answer is incorrect, review the frame you have just studied to see why you were wrong. Remember, minor changes in wording are not counted as mistakes.
6. Keep your study periods brief—about fifteen to thirty minutes in length.

You are now ready to begin "Reading To Understand Science." Good luck!

Joseph A. Fisher

Contents

Part 1
Finding the Principal Idea

To develop skills in understanding the important ideas in scientific materials, we are first going to concentrate on finding the main idea of a written passage. This is usually a general statement which the other sentences in the paragraph expand upon or support. In this book we will call the main ideas of the passages we study *principal ideas*.

The principal idea of a paragraph is not the same thing as the *topic sentence*. The topic sentence is usually the first sentence in a paragraph, and it states the paragraph's subject or *topic*.

The principal idea, however, is a statement (usually *not* in the exact words of the passage) which *summarizes the content* of the passage.

A _____ states in the exact words of the paragraph the topic to be discussed.

Answer: topic sentence

A *principal idea* is a summary statement of the content of a paragraph; it (usually is, usually is not) in the exact words of the passage.

Answer: usually is not

At times it is necessary to combine two or more sentences or ideas in a passage in order to give a full statement of the principal idea. Sometimes the author waits until the end of a paragraph to sum up the main point he is making.

In any case, the principal idea of a passage will be a statement (in your own words) which summarizes the meaning of a passage.

Often in scientific writing we find charts, graphs, tables, and diagrams which present facts or information helpful to the reader in understanding the written material.

Graphic materials are used in scientific writing because they provide _____ in a clear and convenient form.

Answer: facts (information)

In exercises that follow, you will learn to recognize the *principal idea* of scientific passages and the supporting statements for that idea. You will also learn how to read diagrams, graphs, etc. which supply information or facts to clarify the passages.

PHYSICAL SCIENCES

The following passages are taken from textbooks in physics, biology, and chemistry. After each passage, there will be one or more exercises for you to complete. In each case, you can refer to the passage as often as you like.

Let's take an example so that you can get an idea of what this book will try to teach you and how it should be used.

Turn the page and read the passage on "Buoyancy." Then complete the exercises which follow it.

BUOYANCY

Fish are capable of moving toward the surface or into deep water by regulating the quantity of water which they displace and, therefore, the buoyant force. By distending the air bags in their bodies, they can change their volumes and thus change the buoyancy of the water on them. By contracting its air sacs, a fish diminishes its volume, and it sinks. Similarly, a submarine can submerge by taking water into tanks, thus making the submarine heavier than an equal volume of water. It rises from below the surface by blowing or pumping this water out of the tanks.

The first thing to do when reading such a passage is to look for the *principal idea*. We have defined this as a general statement which the other sentences in the passage expand upon or support.

As we said above, the principal idea does not have to be stated in the exact words of the passage. For example, this passage mentions the buoyancy of *fish* and of *submarines*; however, the principal idea could be stated as "buoyancy can be controlled by regulating the amount of water a body displaces." This statement mentions neither *fish* nor *submarines*, both of which are merely *examples* of the general principle of buoyancy.

EXERCISES

1. Fish control buoyancy by regulating the amount of water they displace. This statement:
   a.   Is irrelevant to the principal idea of the passage.
   b.   Is false.
   c.   Is too specific to be the principal idea of the passage.

If you answered *a*, turn to page 6.
If you answered *b*, turn to page 7.
If you answered *c*, turn to page 8.

2. A submarine can submerge by taking water into tanks, thus making the submarine heavier than an equal volume of water.
   This statement:
   a.   Is the principal idea of the passage.
   b.   Is an example used to expand upon the principal idea of the passage.
   c.   Is irrelevant to the principal idea of the passage.

Answer: *b*. Now turn to page 9.

1*a*.   No, this statement is not irrelevant to the principal idea of the passage. We said that the principal idea of this passage was "buoyancy can be controlled by regulating the amount of water a body displaces." The statement about *fish* regulating their buoyancy is a specific example illustrating the principal idea; therefore it is not irrelevant to it.

Go back to page 5, and try exercise 1 again.

1*b*.   No, this statement isn't false. Read the passage again, carefully, and you will see that this statement says essentially the same thing as the first sentence in the paragraph. That first sentence describes the buoyancy of *fish;* it is an illustration or example of the principal idea of buoyancy.

Turn back to page 5, and try exercise 1 again.

1c. Right. This statement about fish is just an example illustrating the principal idea of buoyancy.

Now go back to page 5 and do exercise 2.

Recognizing the principal idea in the buoyancy passage may have seemed difficult at first, but when you realized that the fish and submarines were only examples supporting the principal idea, the author's main intention in the passage probably became clearer.

In this section of the book, you're going to be doing just that—recognizing the principal ideas of scientific passages. Some will be difficult, but they just require a little more concentration. Keep in mind that you will want to clear away the details and examples the author gives and get to the main point he's making, that is, the principal idea.

Read the next passage and the material that follows it.

THEORY OF MAGNETISM

Molecular theory   This theory is based on the assumption that the molecules of a magnetic substance are all individual minute magnets. If a magnetic substance lacks the property of polarity and the power of attraction, it is believed that the many tiny magnets are arranged in a disorganized manner as shown in Fig. 1-1a. However, when a magnetic substance possesses polarity and power of attraction, it is believed that the molecular magnets are arranged in orderly rows, each with its north pole in the same direction as shown in Fig. 1-1b. Also, according to this theory, the molecules in a magnetic substance such as steel, iron, cobalt, or nickel can readily rearrange themselves from a disorganized manner to orderly rows.

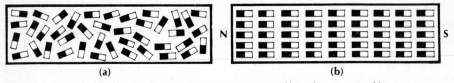

(a)   (b)

Fig. 1-1   The molecular theory of magnetism. **(a)** Unmagnetized bar; **(b)** magnetized bar.

It is often helpful when reading difficult material to break it down into parts in order to understand the author's meaning.

This paragraph can be broken down into four parts:

1. The principal idea of the passage, which is, in this case, the first sentence plus the subtitle: "The molecular theory of magnetism is based on the assumption that the molecules of a magnetic substance are all individual minute magnets."
2. The second sentence: a description of Fig. 1-1*a*—unmagnetized bar.
3. The third sentence: a description of Fig. 1-1*b*—magnetized bar.
4. A concluding statement which applies the molecular theory to certain metals.

The above is a "skeletal" view of the paragraph. If you can break passages down into parts like these—principal idea, descriptions or examples, and concluding statements or applications—you should have no trouble in understanding the passages, even though they contain difficult material.

EXERCISE

A magnetic substance which lacks the property of polarity and the power of attraction contains tiny magnets which are arranged in a disorganized manner.

This statement is:

a. The principal idea of the passage.
b. Too general to be the principal idea of the passage.
c. A description or detail of the theory, that is, too specific to be the principal idea of the passage.

If you answered *a*, turn to page 12.
If you answered *b*, turn to page 13.
If you answered *c*, turn to page 14.

a.   No, this statement is not the principal idea of the passage. It would be a good idea for you to reread the "skeletal" view described on page 11. We stated there that the principal idea of this passage was a general statement of the molecular theory of magnetism.

The sentence in the exercise, on the other hand, is only one part of the theory—it helps to clarify the principal idea of the molecular theory of magnetism.

Go back to page 11, and try the exercise again.

b.   No, this statement isn't too *general* to be the principal idea. If it were too general, it would be vague and would not state anything specific about the paragraph. This statement, however, isn't vague and general. It does state something specific—it describes one aspect of the molecular theory of magnetism.

We said before that the principal idea of this passage stated the molecular theory of magnetism. The statement in exercise 1 helps to clarify the principal idea. Go back to page 11, and try the exercise again.

c.   Very good! That's just what this statement is—a description or elaborating detail of the principal idea—the molecular theory of magnetism.

Turn the page and read the next passage and the material that follows it.

OCEAN'S WORK

The ocean accomplishes most of its work mechanically and only a very minor part chemically. The mechanical work of the ocean is of two different kinds: *erosive* and *depositional*. The depositional work is not only that which is connected with the large quantities of clastic material brought to the ocean by the rivers of the world, but a part (a minor part, of course) is concerned with the formation of deposits from the materials eroded by the waves from the rocks at the seashore. The erosional work of the ocean is concerned also with the process of reducing the size of fragments of rock brought in by the rivers.

This paragraph may seem a bit confusing at first, but let's try to break it up into a "skeletal" form. Again, there are four sentences. The last two are easy: one describes the *depositional* work of the ocean; the other describes the *erosional* work of the ocean. Both sentences *support* or *expand upon* the principal idea.

But what about the first two sentences? Which one is the principal idea?

In this case, we should remember that the principal idea *need not* be in the exact words of the passage. The first sentence is introductory and doesn't contain the complete idea. A combination of the first two sentences will yield a complete statement of the principal idea of the passage.

EXERCISES

1. A complete statement of the principal idea of this passage is:
    a. The ocean accomplishes a minor part of its work chemically, and a major part mechanically through erosion and deposition.
    b. Only a minimum part of the ocean's work is accomplished chemically.
    c. The erosional work of the ocean is concerned with the process of reducing the size of rock fragments brought in by rivers.

Answer: *a.*

2. By now, you should recognize the last two sentences—the one describing *depositional* work of the ocean and the one describing the *erosional* work—merely _____ or _____ the principal idea.

Answer: expand upon, support

Read the selection on page 18.

ENERGY AND ITS CONSERVATION

Energy is defined as the ability or capacity to do work. It occurs in many forms. A swinging hammer can do work by virtue of its motion; energy associated with motion is known as *kinetic energy.* A raised pile driver can do work by virtue of its elevated position; it has what we call *potential energy.* When we buy gasoline, we buy chemical energy. The food we eat provides energy for our living. We purchase electrical energy so our electric motors can do work for us. Energy may exist in the form of electromagnetic radiation; indeed, the earth's primary source of energy lies in the radiation it receives from the sun. Much of physics involves the relationships among the many forms of energy and the transformations from one form to another.

The study of the various forms of energy and of the transformation of one kind of energy into another has led to the statement of a very important principle, known as the *law of conservation of energy: Energy cannot be created or destroyed; it may be transformed from one form into another, but the total amount of energy never changes.*

This principle is one of the great generalizations of physical science.

This time you're on your own. Do the following exercises, and refer to the passage as often as you wish.

EXERCISES \

1. The principal idea of the first paragraph is:
   a. Energy may exist in the form of electromagnetic radiation; indeed, the earth's primary source of energy lies in the radiation it receives from the sun.
   b. A swinging hammer can do work by virtue of its motion; energy associated with motion is known as kinetic energy.
   c. Energy, which occurs in many forms, is defined as the capacity to do work.
   d. A raised pile driver can do work by virtue of its elevated position; it has what we call potential energy.

If you answered a, turn to page 20.
If you answered b, turn to page 21.
If you answered c, turn to page 22.
If you answered d, turn to page 23.

---

2. The principal idea of the second paragraph is:
   a. The law of conservation of energy is a very important principle.
   b. The study of various forms of energy and of the transformation of one kind of energy into another has led to the statement of the law of conservation of energy.
   c. Energy cannot be created or destroyed; it may be transferred from one form into another, but the total amount of energy never changes.

Answer: c. Now turn to page 25.

1*a.*   The answer you chose is indeed a statement about energy, and from the title of this paragraph, we know that energy is the topic under discussion.

However, this statement about electromagnetic radiation describes only one form of energy. Other sentences in the paragraph describe other kinds of energy What we should look for here is a *general* statement about energy which the other sentences expand upon through their description of *kinds* of energy.

Go back to page 19, and try exercise 1 again.

1*b*.   Kinetic energy is *one* kind of energy. But doesn't this paragraph describe *several* kinds? It does indeed, and therefore the principal idea must be a general statement about energy. The sentence about the hammer is merely an illustration of one kind of energy.

Reread the paragraph on page 19, and try exercise 1 again.

1c.   Right! A combination of the first two sentences of the passage gives us a complete statement of the principal idea.

Return to page 19, and do exercise 2.

1*d*. Potential energy is *one* kind of energy. But doesn't this paragraph describe *several* kinds? It does indeed, and therefore the principal idea must be a general statement about energy. The sentence about the pile driver is merely an illustration of one kind of energy.

Reread the paragraph on page 19, and try exercise 1 again.

ORIGIN OF PETROLEUM

The manner of origin of petroleum is still not completely understood, but geologists agree that it formed from animals and plants which lived in the sea at the time the sediments were being deposited. The evidence for this origin is overwhelming. First, petroleum is related to organic matter chemically and in its optical properties. Second, all extensive occurrences of petroleum are associated with sedimentary rocks. Third, large amounts of petroleum are never found except in association with rocks with numerous marine fossils.

As the sediments were deposited, oil was formed by partial decay of animal and plant tissue and was buried in the accumulating sediment. This organic material remained in the sediment as it was altered to rock. Dark shales are likely to be highly bituminous, and oil can be extracted from them, but the present cost is uneconomic. The petroleum in most cases has moved out of the original sediment and has entered porous layers. In these porous layers, it moved upward and accumulated in traps, i.e., in places where impervious material prevented further movement.

Read the accompanying passage, and then do the following exercises. You may refer to the passage as often as you like.

EXERCISES

1. The principal idea of the first paragraph is:
   a. The manner of origin of petroleum is not completely understood, but it is formed from animals and plants which lived in the sea at the time sediments were deposited.
   b. Petroleum is related to organic matter chemically and in its optical properties.
   c. All extensive occurrences of petroleum are associated with sedimentary rocks.
   d. Large amounts of petroleum are never found except in association with rocks with numerous marine fossils.

If you answered a, turn to page 26.
If you answered b, turn to page 27.
If you answered c, turn to page 28.
If you answered d, turn to page 29.

The second paragraph presents several ideas, and it may seem difficult at first to choose the principal idea. The first sentence is not quite enough because another sentence in the paragraph presents a new idea.

The first sentence tells us "oil was formed by partial decay of animal and plant tissue and was buried in the accumulating sediment." However, a later sentence tells us "the petroleum in most cases has moved out of the original sediment and has entered porous layers." Both these ideas are important in the paragraph, and the principal idea, in this case, would have to include them both.

2. We might say, then, that the principal idea of the second paragraph is:
   a. Oil moved upward and accumulated in traps.
   b. Dark shales are likely to be highly bituminous, and oil can be extracted from them.
   c. Oil was formed by partial decay of animal and plant tissue and was buried in sediment; in most cases it has moved out of the original sediment and has entered porous layers.
   d. Oil was formed by partial decay of animal and plant tissue.

Answer: c. Now turn to page 31.

1a.   Yes, this is the principal idea of the passage. You recognized that the other sentences in this paragraph merely support this idea; they back it up in the manner of an argument which the author presents in three sentences with the words "First," "Second," and "Third."

Go back to page 25, and do exercise 2.

1b.   No, this won't qualify as the principal idea of the paragraph. Remember how we broke other paragraphs down to a skeletal form? In this paragraph you should be alert to the way the author states his facts. He is presenting an argument, and to back up his principal idea he uses three supporting facts. He alerts you to this by beginning his sentences with the words "First," "Second," and "Third." These three sentences back up or support his argument.

Reread the paragraph again, slowly, and see if you can recognize its form: first the principal idea is presented, and then three reasons are given to support it.

Return to page 25, and try exercise 1 again.

1*c.*   No, this won't qualify as the principal idea of the paragraph. Remember how we broke other paragraphs down to a skeletal form? In this paragraph you should be alert to the way the author states his facts. He is presenting an argument, and to back up his principal idea he uses three supporting facts. He alerts you to this by beginning his sentences with the words "First," "Second," and "Third." These three sentences back up or support his argument.

Reread the paragraph again, slowly, and see if you can recognize its form: first the principal idea is presented, and then three reasons are given to support it.

Go back to page 25, and try exercise 1 again.

1*d*.   No, this won't qualify as the principal idea of the paragraph. Remember how we broke other paragraphs down to a skeletal form? In this paragraph you should be alert to the way the author states his facts. He is presenting an argument, and to back up his principal idea he uses three supporting facts. He alerts you to this by beginning his sentences with the words "First," "Second," and "Third." These three sentences back up or support his argument.

Reread the paragraph again, slowly, and see if you can recognize its form: first the principal idea is presented, and then three reasons are given to support it.

Go back to page 25, and try exercise 1 again.

WEIGHT VARIATIONS

A man's weight changes as he travels about over the earth. The change is never large—not more than a pound or so at most—but he would have no trouble detecting it with delicate instruments. If he is sufficiently curious, he will discover that there are three distinct types of variation in his weight.

1. Variation with altitude. On a mountaintop he will weigh less than in adjacent valleys. This observation can be explained simply as an effect of changing distance from the earth's center.

2. Variation with latitude. Near the equator he will find his weight a minimum, near the poles a maximum. A little reflection will show two reasons for this variation: (a) the centrifugal force of the earth's rotation, which works against gravity, is greatest at the equator, and (b) points along the equator are farthest from the earth's center, because of the earth's equatorial bulge.

3. Variation with density of subsurface material. In addition to the well-defined variations with latitude and altitude, our investigator will discover erratic minor changes in weight whose explanation is not so obvious. At least in part, these minor variations are due to differences in the rocks immediately below the surface: in regions where the subsurface rocks are unusually heavy, gravity is somewhat greater than in regions underlain by light materials.

Read the accompanying passage, and then answer the questions below. You may refer to the passage as often as you like.

1. The principal idea of the first paragraph is:
   a. It is not difficult to detect variations in weight with delicate instruments.
   b. Man's weight changes as he moves about on earth.
   c. Man's weight never varies more than a pound at most.

Answer: b.

2. The principal idea of the second paragraph is:
   a. Man weighs less on a mountaintop than in a valley.
   b. Man's weight will vary with altitude or distance from the earth's center.
   c. We can observe a difference in weight between mountaintops and adjacent valleys.
   d. We can explain weight variations as an effect of changes in distance from the equator.

Answer: b.

3. The principal idea of the third paragraph is:
   a. Man weighs more at the poles.
   b. Man's weight decreases as he moves toward the equator.
   c. Centrifugal force and the earth's equatorial bulge explain why men weigh less at the equator.
   d. Man's weight changes with variations in latitude.

Answer: d.

WEIGHT VARIATIONS

A man's weight changes as he travels about over the earth. The change is never large—not more than a pound or so at most—but he would have no trouble detecting it with delicate instruments. If he is sufficiently curious, he will discover that there are three distinct types of variation in his weight.

1. Variation with altitude. On a mountaintop he will weigh less than in adjacent valleys. This observation can be explained simply as an effect of changing distance from the earth's center.

2. Variation with latitude. Near the equator he will find his weight a minimum, near the poles a maximum. A little reflection will show two reasons for this variation: (a) the centrifugal force of the earth's rotation, which works against gravity, is greatest at the equator, and (b) points along the equator are farthest from the earth's center, because of the earth's equatorial bulge.

3. Variation with density of subsurface material. In addition to the well-defined variations with latitude and altitude, our investigator will discover erratic minor changes in weight whose explanation is not so obvious. At least in part, these minor variations are due to differences in the rocks immediately below the surface: in regions where the subsurface rocks are unusually heavy, gravity is somewhat greater than in regions underlain by light materials.

4. In the fourth paragraph the principal idea is:
   a. Man's weight varies with the density of subsurface material.
   b. Gravity is greater in regions where the subsurface rocks are unusually heavy.
   c. Where the subsurface rock is light, gravity is not so great.
   d. Major changes in man's weight can be explained by the kind of subsurface rocks.

Answer: *a.*

5. The principal idea discussed in the *entire article* is:
   a. Man's weight on earth varies with altitude, latitude, and density of subsurface materials.
   b. Man's weight varies at the equator because of centrifugal force and the equatorial bulge.
   c. A careful investigation will discover minor variations in man's weight.

Answer: *a.* The principal idea of an entire selection should include the principal ideas of each paragraph within the selection.

TYPES OF EQUILIBRIUM

The equilibrium of a body may be *stable, unstable,* or *neutral* (Fig. 1-2). When a body returns to its original position after being slightly disturbed, the equilibrium is said to be *stable.* A cone standing on its base is an illustration of this type of equilibrium. When this cone is tilted slightly and released, it returns to its original position.

If the cone rests on its vertex, it can be in equilibrium only when its center of gravity lies directly above the vertex. If it is slightly displaced, the cone falls over; it is in *unstable* equilibrium. A body in unstable equilibrium does not return to the original equilibrium position when slightly displaced, but rather moves farther away.

Lastly, a billiard ball resting on a horizontal table is said to be in *neutral* equilibrium. When it is slightly displaced, it neither returns to its former position nor does it go farther away from the initial position. It remains in any position in which it finds itself. A cylinder or a cone lying on its side on a horizontal surface is also in neutral equilibrium.

The position of the center of gravity is of paramount importance in determining the stability of a body. The lower the center of gravity, the greater the stability of the body and the more difficult it is to overturn it. The body becomes unstable as soon as the vertical line through its center of gravity falls outside its base. The leaning Tower of Pisa remains in stable equilibrium because, in spite of its leaning, the line of action of the weight falls inside the base.

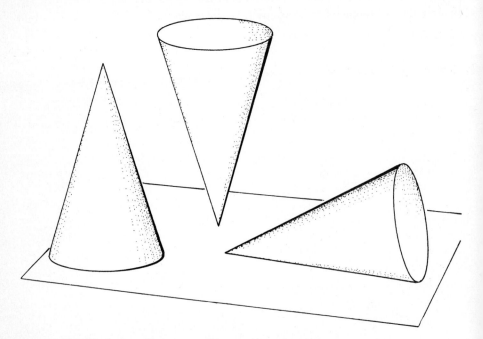

Fig. 1-2   Three kinds of equilibrium are *stable, unstable,* and *neutral.*

Read the accompanying selection, and then answer the following questions. You may refer to the material as often as you wish.

1. The principal idea of the first paragraph is:
   a. When a body returns to its original position after being slightly disturbed, the equilibrium is said to be stable.
   b. A cone standing on its base is in stable equilibrium.
   c. When a cone is on its base and tilted slightly, it is in stable equilibrium.
   d. A cone may be in stable, unstable, or neutral equilibrium.

Answer: *a*. (The statements about cones are merely examples of the principal idea.)

2. The principal idea of the second paragraph is:
   a. A cone can only be in equilibrium when its center of gravity is directly above its vertex.
   b. A body in unstable equilibrium does not return to its original position when slightly displaced.
   c. A cone resting on its vertex will fall over if slightly displaced.
   d. A cone cannot remain in a state of unstable equilibrium.

Answer: *b*.

3. The principal idea expressed in the third paragraph is:
   a. A billiard ball resting on a horizontal table is in a state of neutral equilibrium.
   b. A billiard ball remains in the position in which it finds itself.
   c. A body in neutral equilibrium neither returns nor moves farther away from its initial position.
   d. A cylinder or cone lying on its side is in neutral equilibrium.

Answer: *c*. Again, cones and billiard balls are used as *examples* of neutral equilibrium.

TYPES OF EQUILIBRIUM

The equilibrium of a body may be *stable, unstable,* or *neutral* (Fig. 1-2). When a body returns to its original position after being slightly disturbed, the equilibrium is said to be *stable.* A cone standing on its base is an illustration of this type of equilibrium. When this cone is tilted slightly and released, it returns to its original position.

If the cone rests on its vertex, it can be in equilibrium only when its center of gravity lies directly above the vertex. If it is slightly displaced, the cone falls over; it is in *unstable* equilibrium. A body in unstable equilibrium does not return to the original equilibrium position when slightly displaced, but rather moves farther away.

Lastly, a billiard ball resting on a horizontal table is said to be in *neutral* equilibrium. When it is slightly displaced, it neither returns to its former position nor does it go farther away from the initial position. It remains in any position in which it finds itself. A cylinder or a cone lying on its side on a horizontal surface is also in neutral equilibrium.

The position of the center of gravity is of paramount importance in determining the stability of a body. The lower the center of gravity, the greater the stability of the body and the more difficult it is to overturn it. The body becomes unstable as soon as the vertical line through its center of gravity falls outside its base. The leaning Tower of Pisa remains in stable equilibrium because, in spite of its leaning, the line of action of the weight falls inside the base.

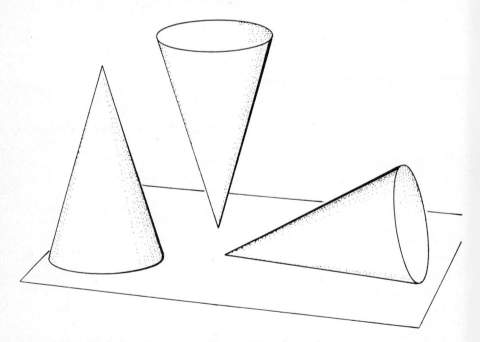

Fig. 1-2 Three kinds of equilibrium are *stable, unstable,* and *neutral.*

4. The principal idea of the fourth paragraph is:
   a. The lower the center of gravity, the greater the stability of the body.
   b. A body becomes unstable as soon as the vertical line through its center of gravity falls outside its base.
   c. The Tower of Pisa is stable because the line of action of its weight falls inside the base.
   d. The position of the center of gravity is of paramount importance in determining the stability of the body.

Answer: d.

5. The principal idea of the *entire selection* is:
   a. A body may be in stable, unstable, or neutral equilibrium depending on the position of its center of gravity.
   b. The lower the center of gravity of a body, the greater its stability and the more difficult it is to overturn it.
   c. When a body is displaced and neither returns to its original position nor moves farther from the original position, it is in neutral equilibrium.
   d. The equilibrium of a body may be stable, unstable, or neutral.

Answer: a. This statement includes the principal ideas of all four paragraphs.

THE ELEMENTS

The analyses of air, water, and a diamond have given different results. Air is composed of oxygen, nitrogen, and other gases. It is a mixture. Water is composed of hydrogen and oxygen. It is a compound. The diamond, on the other hand, is pure carbon. It is an element. No chemical method can divide it into simpler substances.

In the next few passages, first choose the principal idea from a list of four statements. Then match the three incorrect statements with a list of reasons telling why each statement is *not* the principal idea. The reasons will be listed as "Too general," "Too specific," and "Irrelevant."

"Too general" means that the statement given is too vague and does not fully express the principal idea of the passage.

"Too specific" means that the statement given is merely a detail or supporting fact in the paragraph, rather than the principal idea.

"Irrelevant" means that the statement given covers ideas not actually presented in the paragraph.

Read the accompanying passage on "The Elements," and then answer the questions below. You may refer to the passage as often as you like.

1. The principal idea of the paragraph is:
   a. The analyses of air, water, and a diamond have given different results.
   b. While compounds and mixtures can be divided into simpler parts, an element cannot be divided this way.
   c. The diamond, on the other hand, is pure carbon.
   d. Air and water are necessary for human life, while diamonds are not.

Answer: *b.*

---

2. Now match each statement below with the reason that it is *not* the principal idea.
   _____   1. The analyses of air, water, and a diamond have given different results.
   _____   2. The diamond, on the other hand, is pure carbon.
   _____   3. Air and water are necessary for human life, while diamonds are not.

Reasons
a. Too general.
b. Too specific.
c. Irrelevant.

Answers: 1. *a.*
          2. *b.*
          3. *c.* This fact is not mentioned in the passage.

PROTEIN SENSITIVITY

As a result of their complicated geometric makeup, proteins are extremely sensitive to chemical and physical influences. Excessive heat, pressure, electricity, heavy metals, and many other agents produce protein denaturation: cross-linkages within the folded amino acid chain are broken, the exquisite geometry of arrangement is disarranged or destroyed, and the molecule collapses. Extreme disarrangement is spoken of as **coagulation**. In living matter, a protein in a slightly denatured state may sometimes revert to the **native** state, and vice versa. But once coagulated, like boiled egg white, a protein usually cannot be restored to its native form. Cellular death is sometimes a result of irreversible protein coagulation.

Read the accompanying passage, and then answer these questions about it. You may refer to the paragraph as often as you wish.

1. The principal idea of the paragraph is:
   - *a.* Proteins have a complex geometric makeup.
   - *b.* In living matter, a protein in a slightly denatured state may sometimes revert to the natural state.
   - *c.* Due to its complex geometric structure, protein is extremely sensitive to chemical and physical influences.
   - *d.* Proteins can be compared to boiled egg whites.

Answer: *c.*

2. Match the following statements with the reasons which best explain why they are *not* good statements of the principal idea of the passage.
   - _____ 1. In living matter, a protein in a slightly denatured state may sometimes revert to the native state.
   - _____ 2. Proteins have a complex geometric makeup.
   - _____ 3. Proteins can be compared to boiled egg whites.

Reasons
- *a.* Too general.
- *b.* Too specific.
- *c.* Irrelevant.

Answers: 1. *b.*
           2. *a.*
           3. *c.*

PROTEIN SPECIFICITY

Indeed, no two types of living organisms contain identical proteins (although the same *categories* of proteins may be present). This is not the case for carbohydrates or fats. A given complex carbohydrate, for example, is the same whether we obtain it from mushrooms or mangoes, from mice or from men. A given fat, similarly, is the same fat regardless of where we find it. This is not so for proteins, however. Even two sister plants have slightly different proteins, and the more unrelated two organisms are evolutionally, the greater are the structural differences between their proteins. We say that proteins have a high degree of specificity: the proteins of a given living unit have a unit-"specific" character; i.e., they are unique for that unit.

Protein specificity has major consequences, some of which are well known. For example, transfer of protein from one organism into the living substance of another amounts to the introduction of foreign bodies, and disease may result. Thus, the proteins of plant pollen may produce allergy in man. Bacteria, partly because their proteins differ from those of other organisms, may produce many diseases if they infect given hosts. A number of other significant consequences of protein specificity will be discussed later.

Read the passage, and then answer these questions. You may refer to the passage as often as you wish.

1. The principal idea of the first paragraph is:
   a. Living organisms may not contain identical proteins.
   b. A given complex carbohydrate is the same whether we obtain it from mushrooms or mangoes, from mice or men.
   c. Living matter contains fats, carbohydrates, and proteins.
   d. Proteins have a high degree of specificity; they have a unit-"specific" character; that is, they are unique for that unit.

Answer: *d.*

2. Match the following:
   _____ 1. A given complex carbohydrate is the same whether we obtain it from mushrooms or mangoes, from mice or men.
   _____ 2. Living matter contains fats, carbohydrates, and proteins.
   _____ 3. Living organisms may not contain identical proteins.

Reasons
a. Too general to be the principal idea.
b. Too specific to be the principal idea.
c. Irrelevant to the principal idea.

Answers: 1. *b.*
          2. *c.* This is not stated in the passage.
          3. *a.*

3. The principal idea of the second paragraph is:
   a. Protein specificity has major consequences.
   b. Transfer of protein from one organism to another is a difficult process.
   c. Proteins of plant pollen may produce allergy in man.
   d. Protein specificity has major consequences, as in the transfer of protein from one organism to another.

Answer: *d.*

PROTEIN SPECIFICITY

Indeed, no two types of living organisms contain identical proteins (although the same *categories* of proteins may be present). This is not the case for carbohydrates or fats. A given complex carbohydrate, for example, is the same whether we obtain it from mushrooms or mangoes, from mice or from men. A given fat, similarly, is the same fat regardless of where we find it. This is not so for proteins, however. Even two sister plants have slightly different proteins, and the more unrelated two organisms are evolutionarily, the greater are the structural differences between their proteins. We say that proteins have a high degree of specificity: the proteins of a given living unit have a unit-"specific" character; i.e., they are unique for that unit.

Protein specificity has major consequences, some of which are well known. For example, transfer of protein from one organism into the living substance of another amounts to the introduction of foreign bodies, and disease may result. Thus, the proteins of plant pollen may produce allergy in man. Bacteria, partly because their proteins differ from those of other organisms, may produce many diseases if they infect given hosts. A number of other significant consequences of protein specificity will be discussed later.

4. Match the following:

——— 1. Transfer of proteins from one organism to another is a difficult process.

——— 2. Protein specificity has major consequences.

——— 3. Proteins of plant pollen may produce allergy in man.

Reasons

a. Too general to be the principal idea.

b. Too specific to be the principal idea.

c. Irrelevant to the principal idea.

Answers: 1. *c.*

2. *a.*

3. *b.*

IONIZATION

When they are dissolved in water, as in living matter, some kinds of molecules do, and some do not, remain intact. Those which do not remain intact break up, or *dissociate*, into two or more electrically charged atoms or groups of atoms, called **ions.** For example, table salt, sodium chloride (NaCl), is an ionizing substance. In cells or in water generally, it dissociates into a positively charged sodium ion (Na^+) and a negatively charged chloride ion (Cl^-).

$$NaCl \longrightarrow Na^+ + Cl^-$$

| sodium | sodium | chloride |
| chloride | ion | ion |

The solution now contains an equal number of such positive and negative ions, and it therefore remains electrically neutral as a whole. Electric neutrality is always preserved in solutions of ionized substances. But the presence of ions, rather than of whole molecules, makes possible the conduction of electric currents through the solution. Substances which ionize are also called **electrolytes;** those which do not ionize, **nonelectrolytes.** Living matter contains both kinds.

Read the accompanying passage carefully, and then answer the questions below. You may refer to the passage as often as you like.

1. The principal idea of the first paragraph is:
   a. When dissolved in water, some kinds of molecules do not remain intact, but dissociate into two or more electrically charged atoms called ions.
   b. In water, sodium chloride dissociates into a positively charged sodium ion and a negatively charged chloride ion.
   c. Molecules, when they dissolve in water, may or may not dissociate into positive and negative ions.
   d. It is not a good idea to dissolve table salt ($NaCl$) in water.

Answer: *a.*

2. Match the following:
   ——— 1. In water, sodium chloride dissolves into a positively charged sodium ion and a negatively charged chloride ion.
   ——— 2. Molecules, when they dissolve in water, may or may not dissociate into positive and negative ions.
   ——— 3. It is not a good idea to dissolve table salt ($NaCl$) in water.

Reasons
a. Too general to be the principal idea of the first paragraph.
b. Too specific to be the principal idea of the first paragraph.
c. Irrelevant to the principal idea.

Answers: 1. *b.*
            2. *a.*
            3. *c.*

IONIZATION

When they are dissolved in water, as in living matter, some kinds of molecules do, and some do not, remain intact. Those which do not remain intact break up, or *dissociate,* into two or more electrically charged atoms or groups of atoms, called **ions.** For example, table salt, sodium chloride (NaCl), is an ionizing substance. In cells or in water generally, it dissociates into a positively charged sodium ion (Na^+) and a negatively charged chloride ion (Cl^-):

$$NaCl \longrightarrow Na^+ \quad + \quad Cl^-$$

sodium	*sodium*	*chloride*
chloride	*ion*	*ion*

The solution now contains an equal number of such positive and negative ions, and it therefore remains electrically neutral as a whole. Electric neutrality is always preserved in solutions of ionized substances. But the presence of ions, rather than of whole molecules, makes possible the conduction of electric currents through the solution. Substances which ionize are also called **electrolytes;** those which do not ionize, **nonelectrolytes.** Living matter contains both kinds.

3. The principal idea of the second paragraph is:
   a. Substances which ionize are called electrolytes; those which do not are called nonelectrolytes.
   b. Some solutions contain an equal number of positive and negative ions.
   c. Ionized substances preserve electric neutrality.
   d. Ionized solutions are always electrically neutral, but the ions make possible the conduction of electrical currents through the solution.

Answer: *d.*

4. Match the following:
   _____ 1. Substances which ionize are called electrolytes; those which do not are called nonelectrolytes.
   _____ 2. Some solutions contain an equal number of positive and negative ions.
   _____ 3. Ionized substances preserve electric neutrality.

Reasons
a. Too general to be the principal idea.
b. Too specific to be the principal idea.
c. Irrelevant to the principal idea.

Answers: 1. *b.*
          2. *c.*
          3. *a.*

IONIZATION

When they are dissolved in water, as in living matter, some kinds of molecules do, and some do not, remain intact. Those which do not remain intact break up, or *dissociate*, into two or more electrically charged atoms or groups of atoms, called **ions.** For example, table salt, sodium chloride (NaCl), is an ionizing substance. In cells or in water generally, it dissociates into a positively charged sodium ion (Na^+) and a negatively charged chloride ion (Cl^-):

$$NaCl \longrightarrow Na^+ \quad + \quad Cl^-$$

sodium chloride	sodium ion	chloride ion

The solution now contains an equal number of such positive and negative ions, and it therefore remains electrically neutral as a whole. Electric neutrality is always preserved in solutions of ionized substances. But the presence of ions, rather than of whole molecules, makes possible the conduction of electric currents through the solution. Substances which ionize are also called **electrolytes;** those which do not ionize, **nonelectrolytes.** Living matter contains both kinds.

5. The principal idea of the *entire selection* may be best stated as:
   a. When dissolved in water, some molecules dissociate into two or more electrically charged atoms called ions which form an electrically neutral solution which can conduct electric current.
   b. When sodium chloride is dissolved in water its molecules dissociate into positively charged sodium ions and negatively charged chloride ions forming an electrically neutral solution through which electric current can pass.
   c. Table salt (NaCl) is not a nonelectrolyte.
   d. Substances which dissociate in water form ions which allow electric current to pass through the solution.

Answer: *a.*

6. Which response in question 5 is unsuitable because it is too specific?

Answer: *b.*

7. Which response in question 5 is unsuitable because it is irrelevant?

Answer: *c.*

8. Which response in question 5 is unsuitable because it is too general?

Answer: *d.*

MOVEMENT THROUGH MEMBRANES

Diffusion   When we detect the odor of an orange being peeled, we have an example of the *diffusion,* or spreading, of gases through the air. Substances can also diffuse through a liquid medium, as when a crystal of copper sulfate or some potassium permanganate is dropped into water and the color can be seen to spread away from its source. The diffusing substance goes into solution in water, which in this case is its *solvent.* The dissolved substance in solution is the *solute.* The molecules of the solute spread slowly from the area of greatest concentration and eventually spread evenly and reach an equilibrium throughout the solvent (Fig. 1-3).

Osmosis   Molecules of a great variety of substances move in and out through cell membranes, but not all molecules are able to pass through. The membrane is called *semipermeable* or *selectively permeable.* In general, cell membranes must contain the protoplasm of the cell but permit oxygen to pass in and carbon dioxide to pass out. Nutritive materials also must enter the cell, and excretory materials must be disposed of.

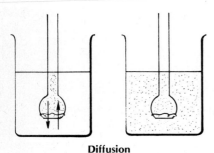   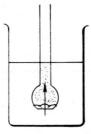   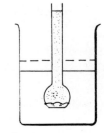

Diffusion   **Osmosis**

Fig. 1-3   Movement through membranes.

In the next few exercises, write *in your own words* the principal idea of each passage on the lines provided. You may refer to the passage if you wish. Check your answer with the one given below the question. They should be approximately the same, though of course they won't be identical.

1. The principal idea of the first paragraph is:

_____

_____

_____

Answer: Diffusion allows molecules of a solute to spread from the area of greatest concentration and eventually spread evenly and reach an equilibrium throughout the solvent.

2. The principal idea of the second paragraph is:

_____

_____

_____

Answer: In osmosis, molecules of a great variety of substances move in and out through cell membranes which are semipermeable or selectively permeable.

FUNCTIONAL CHARACTERISTICS

Plant or animal, unicellular or multicellular, every organism is a variation on the functional themes elaborated a few billion years ago. All organisms perform the various activities which the very first cells had already performed. These activities may be grouped into two broad categories of functions, namely, **metabolism** and **self-perpetuation.**

Metabolism comprises the functions of **nutrition, respiration,** and **synthesis,** and all processes associated with these three. Nutrition provides the raw materials for life. Respiration extracts energy from some of the raw materials. With a portion of this energy, synthesis transforms the other raw materials into structural components of living matter. The remainder of the energy and all the structural components then make self-perpetuation possible.

In principle, metabolism occurs also in inanimate machines. A machine may be designed to take on "nourishment" in the form of fuel and raw materials. The fuel may provide operating energy, and with it, the raw materials may then be processed into nuts, bolts, shafts, and other structural components out of which such a machine is built. If, for one reason or another, any one of these processes should stop, the machine would cease to operate even though it is still whole and intact. Similarly, if a metabolic function of an organism is stopped, the organism becomes nonoperational and dies.

1. The principal idea of the first paragraph is:

_____

_____

_____

———————————————————————

Answer: Every organism is a variation on the functional themes of metabolism and self-perpetuation.

_____

2. The principal idea of the second paragraph is:

_____

_____

_____

———————————————————————

Answer: Metabolism comprises the functions of nutrition, respiration, and snythesis, and all processes associated with these three.

_____

3. The principal idea of the third paragraph is:

_____

_____

_____

———————————————————————

Answer: In principle, metabolism occurs in inanimate machines, as a machine can take "nourishment" in the form of fuel which provides operating energy.

_____

THE ECOSYSTEM

Animals and plants, as they exist in nature, are part of an ecological system, or **ecosystem** (EK·o·sis·tem). Ecosystem is a dynamic concept. It includes all the ways individual organisms interact with one another and with their nonliving environment. The predators, the prey, the producers, the decomposers, the energy sources, and the matter from which living substances are derived are all involved in the ecosystem. One could say that the word *ecosystem* just means "living nature" were it not for the fact that "nature" has so many different meanings.

An ecosystem may be in a square meter of prairie, the edge of a pond, a tide pool, a few cubic meters of surface water of the ocean, or a balanced aquarium. None of these is a complete and independent ecosystem—not even the whole world is. Perhaps the balanced aquarium comes closest of any on the list; all it needs is light and a proper temperature. The tide pool, on the other hand, is influenced by what occurs in the nearby ocean and on the shore. There are no sharp boundaries to the ecosystem that exists in a tide pool—or to most other ecosystems.

1. The principal idea of the first paragraph is:

_____

_____

_____

Answer: The concept of ecosystem includes all the ways individual organisms interact with one another and with their nonliving environment.

2. The principal idea of the second paragraph is:

_____

_____

_____

Answer: An ecosystem is never complete and independent, and most ecosystems lack sharp boundaries.

Turn to page 59 and continue work.

SOCIAL SCIENCES

We have separated this section, "Social Sciences," from the previous section, "Physical Sciences," because the nature of the reading is somewhat different. You are still going to look for the principal idea of each passage, but first you should be aware of the difference between principal ideas of the physical sciences and those of the social sciences.

In the physical sciences (physics, chemistry, biology, etc.) the principal ideas which we found in the passages were scientifically provable. Scientists had performed certain experiments under controlled conditions and the results were accepted into the large body of scientific fact.

In the social sciences, however, the principal ideas you will be finding will be of a slightly different kind. Concepts of the family or theories of economics are found through surveys and studies which produce *statistics* and *percentages*. From these, conclusions are drawn. The principal ideas in the following passages will consist mainly of this kind of conclusion.

In a subject like history, one might say that there is a certain body of facts which are provable and are not merely statistics. This is so, but the conclusions drawn from a passage of a history text are not the same as the indisputable conclusions of a scientific experiment.

For example, our first passage is about "The Spanish in the New World." The first sentence states a historical fact; the rest of the paragraph considers some possible motives or causes of colonization. As you read the paragraph and answer the questions that follow it, remember that you are now dealing not with indisputable *scientific facts*, but with theories and ideas. The method for finding the principal idea is the same: decide what the paragraph is about, which sentences are merely supporting details, and then construct a statement which sums up the principal idea of the passage.

The exercises will be slightly different from those used in the previous section. You will, as before, choose the principal idea from four given statements. Then you will match the incorrect statements with the reasons that they are *not* the principal idea ("too general," "too specific," and "irrelevant"). However, in these exercises you will sometimes also be asked if a statement is true or false. Occasionally, too, you will be given a sentence to complete by filling in the blanks.

THE SPANISH IN THE NEW WORLD

Sixteenth-century maps show vast territories in Asia, Africa, and the New World claimed by various European nations. In fact, the Europeans often claimed far more than they ever hoped to control. For the most part, they merely hoped to monopolize trade with the regions they claimed; they did not expect to conquer these people or make them subjects.

Read the accompanying passage, and then answer the following questions. You may refer to the selection as often as you like.

1. What is the principal idea of this passage?
    a. Sixteenth-century maps show vast territories in Asia, Africa, and the New World claimed by various European countries.
    b. European nations traded extensively in the sixteenth century.
    c. European nations hoped to monopolize trade with the regions they claimed throughout the world.
    d. Europe, Spain, and France did not expect to conquer the people of the territories they claimed throughout the world or make them loyal subjects.

Answer: c.

2. Match the following:
    _____ 1. Sixteenth-century maps show vast territories in Asia, Africa, and the New World claimed by various European countries.
    _____ 2. European nations traded extensively in the sixteenth century.
    _____ 3. Europe, Spain, and France did not expect to conquer the people of the territories they claimed throughout the world or make them loyal subjects.

Reasons
a. Too general to be the principal idea.
b. Too specific to be the principal idea.
c. Irrelevant to the principal idea.

Answers: 1. a.
           2. c.
           3. b.

SELF-IMAGE

Although a child may be intelligent and quite capable physically, he may, if reared by indifferent parents and subjected to constant criticism and belittlement, learn to perceive himself as an inadequate, undesirable person. Most of us have known people who constantly underrate their own performance. By the same token, we have also known people with a grossly exaggerated view of their accomplishments and capabilities. Children surrounded by an admiring and doting family who praise even poor performance excessively are often found to have excessive self-evaluations.

Read the accompanying passage, and then answer the questions below. You may refer to the passage as often as you like.

1. The principal idea stated in the paragraph is:
   a. Some people have a grossly exaggerated view of their own accomplishments and capabilities.
   b. If reared by indifferent parents and subjected to constant criticism, a child will perceive himself as inadequate and inferior; if the child is reared by admiring and doting parents, he will have an exaggerated opinion of his abilities.
   c. A child's intellectual and physical capabilities determine his self-concept.
   d. The attitude of parents toward a child has profound influence on his self-concept.

Answer: d.

2. If reared by indifferent parents and subjected to constant criticism, a child will perceive himself as inadequate and inferior; if the child is reared by admiring and doting parents, he will have an exaggerated opinion of his abilities.
   This is not a good statement of the principal idea of the passage because it is:
   a. Too detailed.
   b. Irrelevant.
   c. Too general.

Answer: a.

3. A child's intellectual and physical capabilities determine his self-concept.
   This statement is:
   a. Too general to be a good statement of the principal idea.
   b. Inadequate as the principal idea of the passage because it is untrue.
   c. Too specific to be the principal idea of the passage.

Answer: b.

THE FAMILY

The family is the most permanent and the most pervasive of all social institutions. There is no human society in which some form of the family does not appear nor, so far as we know, has there ever been such a society. All societies, both large and small, primitive and civilized, ancient and modern, have institutionalized the process of procreation of the species and the rearing of the young. As in the case of most social institutions, it is idle to inquire into origins. No one knows, or can know, how or when the family began, if indeed the concept of beginning has any meaning in this connection. It is safe to surmise, however, that the family in some form will always be with us, that as far into the future as the mind can imagine, the family will continue to be a central and indeed a nuclear component of society. There may be no families in utopia, and none in paradise, but the planet we know best will probably always contain them.

Read the accompanying selection, and then answer the questions below. You may refer to the passage as often as you like.

1. The principal idea of this passage is:
   a. There is no human society in which some form of the family does not appear nor, so far as we know, has there ever been such a society.
   b. All societies, both large and small, primitive and civilized, ancient and modern, have institutionalized the process of procreation of the species and the rearing of the young.
   c. Though the family has appeared in some form in the past, it is safe to surmise that at some time in the future the family will not be the nuclear component of society.
   d. The family is the most permanent and the most pervasive of all social institutions: as far as we know, it has always existed in society, and it will probably always exist in the future.

Answer: *d.*

2. Match the following:
   _____ 1. There is no human society in which some form of the family does not appear nor, so far as we know, has there ever been such a society.
   _____ 2. All societies, both large and small, primitive and civilized, ancient and modern, have institutionalized the process of procreation of the species and the rearing of the young.
   _____ 3. Though the family has appeared in some form in the past, it is safe to surmise that at some time in the future the family will not be the nuclear component of society.

Reasons
a. Too general to be the principal idea.
b. Untrue.
c. Too specific to be the principal idea.

Answers: 1. *c.*
          2. *a.*
          3. *b.*

GREEK PHILOSOPHERS AND TEACHERS

There were many great teachers and philosophers in Greece, but three were particularly important: Socrates, Plato, and Aristotle. Socrates, the greatest Greek teacher, was born in Athens about 469 B.C. He was a loyal, and at all times fearless, citizen of Athens. In the later years of his life, he spent much of his time wandering about the city, asking questions of the people he met. He asked questions about right and wrong, about good and bad government, and about the gods and goddesses.

In particular, Socrates asked questions about the meaning of words which people were accustomed to using. When anyone used such words as justice or truth, Socrates was likely to ask, "What do you mean by justice? What do you mean by truth?" Whatever answer might be given, he would then ask another question. By using this "Socratic method," he taught men to be critical of themselves and their ideas, and to accept nothing without thought and questioning.

Read the accompanying passage, and then answer the questions below. You may refer to the passage as often as you like.

1. The principal idea of the first paragraph is:
    a. The Greeks had many great teachers and philosophers, but the three most famous were Socrates, Plato, and Aristotle.
    b. Socrates, the greatest Greek teacher, was born in Athens about 469 B.C.
    c. The Greeks are known for the great number of teachers and philosophers which they produced.
    d. Socrates spent his time in his later years wandering about the city of Athens asking questions of people he met.

Answer: *b.* (While the paragraph mentions three great Greek philosophers, it describes only one of them: Socrates.)

2. Match the following:
    _____ 1. The Greeks had many great teachers and philosophers, but the three most famous were Socrates, Plato, and Aristotle.
    _____ 2. The Greeks are known for the great number of teachers and philosophers which they produced.
    _____ 3. Socrates spent his time in his later years wandering about the city of Athens asking questions of the people he met.

Reasons
    a. Too general to be the principal idea of the paragraph.
    b. Too specific to be the principal idea of the paragraph.
    c. Irrelevant to the principal idea of the paragraph.

Answers: 1. *a.*
             2. *c.*
             3. *b.*

3. Complete this statement of the principal idea of the second paragraph:
    Socrates used the _____ to teach men to be critical and accept nothing without _____ and _____

Answers: Socratic method, thought, questioning.

GREEK PHILOSOPHERS AND TEACHERS

There were many great teachers and philosophers in Greece, but three were particularly important: Socrates, Plato, and Aristotle. Socrates, the greatest Greek teacher, was born in Athens about 469 B.C. He was a loyal, and at all times fearless, citizen of Athens. In the later years of his life, he spent much of his time wandering about the city, asking questions of the people he met. He asked questions about right and wrong, about good and bad government, and about the gods and goddesses.

In particular, Socrates asked questions about the meaning of words which people were accustomed to using. When anyone used such words as justice or truth, Socrates was likely to ask, "What do you mean by justice? What do you mean by truth?" Whatever answer might be given, he would then ask another question. By using this "Socratic method," he taught men to be critical of themselves and their ideas, and to accept nothing without thought and questioning.

4. The principal idea of the *entire selection* is:
   a. All great Greek philosophers used the Socratic method.
   b. Socrates asked many questions about the meanings of words.
   c. The method of teaching used by Socrates, the greatest of Greek philosophers and teachers, is called the "Socratic method."
   d. Greece produced many great teachers and philosophers, the most important of whom were Socrates, Plato, and Aristotle.

Answer: *c.*

VOCABULARY

Earlier we stressed the enormous number of symbols and signals made available by a language. Actually, the English language contains well over a half-million words. Probably no one knows all these words, even if the thousands of technical words used only by scholars to denote their materials and concepts are omitted. In fact, most people have a surprisingly small vocabulary—considering the number of words available—and can expand this vocabulary only under special conditions.

The number of words a person knows is usually considered to be his vocabulary; but to be more accurate, we must recognize that each person has not just one, but rather several vocabularies. First of all is the vocabulary he can *recognize*. This is almost always considerably larger than the one he can speak or write. When we traced the development of language in the child, we pointed out that children can understand and recognize words before they can use them—at least in a way that others can understand—and a similar difference continues throughout life between what is recognizable and what is usable.

Read the accompanying passage, and then answer the questions below. You may refer to the passage as often as you like.

1. The principal idea of the first paragraph is:
   a. The English language contains well over 1½ million words.
   b. Even if we omit technical words, probably no one knows all the words of the English language.
   c. Most people know the words they need in daily speech.
   d. Most people have surprisingly small vocabularies and expand them only under special conditions.

Answer: d.

2. Match the following:
   _____ 1. The English language contains well over 1½ million words.
   _____ 2. Even if we omit technical words, probably no one knows all the words of the English language.
   _____ 3. Most people know the words they need in daily speech.

Reasons
a. Irrelevant to the principal idea of the paragraph.
b. Untrue.
c. Too specific to be the principal idea of the paragraph.

Answers: 1. b.
          2. c.
          3. a.

3. Complete this statement of the principal idea of the second paragraph: A person's true vocabulary consists of words he can _____ as well as words he can _____

Answer: use (speak, write), recognize.

VOCABULARY

Earlier we stressed the enormous number of symbols and signals made available by a language. Actually, the English language contains well over a half-million words. Probably no one knows all these words, even if the thousands of technical words used only by scholars to denote their materials and concepts are omitted. In fact, most people have a surprisingly small vocabulary—considering the number of words available—and can expand this vocabulary only under special conditions.

The number of words a person knows is usually considered to be his vocabulary; but to be more accurate, we must recognize that each person has not just one, but rather several vocabularies. First of all is the vocabulary he can *recognize*. This is almost always considerably larger than the one he can speak or write. When we traced the development of language in the child, we pointed out that children can understand and recognize words before they can use them—at least in a way that others can understand—and a similar difference continues throughout life between what is recognizable and what is usable.

4. Which of these is the best statement of the principal idea of the *entire selection?*

   a. Most people have surprisingly limited vocabularies which they expand only under specific conditions.
   b. Most people's vocabularies are limited; their vocabularies are developed only under specific conditions and contain both words which they can recognize and words they can use correctly.
   c. A person's vocabulary consists of all those words he can recognize.
   d. Probably no one knows all the words in the English language—even if we omit thousands of purely technical words.

Answer: *b.*

ECONOMIC DEMAND

A fundamental characteristic of demand is this: As price falls, the corresponding quantity demanded rises, or, alternatively, as price increases, the corresponding quantity demanded falls. In short, there is an *inverse* relationship between price and quantity demanded. Economists have labeled this inverse relationship the *law of demand*. Upon what foundation does this law rest? There are many levels on which the case can be argued, but it is sufficient for our purposes to rest the case on common sense and simple observation. People ordinarily *do* buy more of a given product at a low price than they do at a high price. To consumers price is an obstacle which deters them from buying. The higher this obstacle, the less of a product they will buy; the lower the price obstacle, the more they will buy. In other words, a high price discourages consumers from buying, and a low price encourages them to buy. The simple fact that businessmen have sales is concrete evidence of their belief in the law of demand. Bargain, or sales, days are based on the law of demand.

Read the accompanying passage, and then answer the questions below. You may refer to the passage as often as you wish.

1. Complete this statement of the principal idea of the passage:

The law of demand is _____

_____

_____

Answer: an inverse relationship between price and quantity demanded.

2. To consumers price is an obstacle which deters them from buying. This statement is *not* the principal idea because it is_____

Answer: too specific.

MOTIVES FOR ENGLISH COLONIES

By the early seventeenth century, mercantilism had been generally accepted as an economic theory. Seeking a favorable balance of trade, Englishmen saw two ways in which overseas possessions, or colonies, might make their country prosperous. The most direct way was to find gold and silver. The Spaniards had done that, and Englishmen hoped they could do the same. The second way was to obtain products from the colony that otherwise would have to be bought from foreign nations.

There was another reason why thoughtful Englishmen were interested in colonies. An increase in sheep raising caused a rise in the number of unemployed agricultural workers. It was believed that these men could be recruited by colonizing companies and sent to the colonies.

Such were the reasons that made the rulers of England, the nobles, and the merchants interested in founding colonies. But the motives of the emigrants for settling in the colonies were different. In the sixteenth century, when the Anglican Church had been established, all Englishmen had to worship according to the Anglican beliefs. Catholics, and other Protestants, called Separatists, were denied freedom of worship. Many Separatists, and particularly the Pilgrims, believing in discarding all of the outward aspects of Catholicism such as rituals and bishops, sought religious freedom in the new colonies. English Quakers, Presbyterians, Baptists, Catholics, Jews, and French Huguenots followed the earlier colonists into the North American settlements or founded their own.

In addition, because of the war between Holland and Spain, the English export wool trade was disrupted. This falloff in trade, plus the general overpopulation, led many farmers and artisans to hope that in a colony they could make a better living than at home.

1. The principal idea of the first paragraph is:
   a. The English used their colonies to provide them with gold and silver and to provide them with products which they would otherwise have to buy from foreign nations.
   b. The English sought a balance of trade with their colonies.
   c. The English hoped to obtain gold and silver from their colonies.
   d. The Spaniards as well as the English used their colonies' resources.

Answer: *a.*

2. Complete this statement of the principal idea of the second paragraph: It was believed that the unemployed agricultural workers in England could be _____

Answer: recruited by colonizing companies and sent to the colonies.

3. The principal idea of the third paragraph is:

_____

_____

_____

Answer: The emigrants who settled in the colonies were seeking religious freedom.

MOTIVES FOR ENGLISH COLONIES

By the early seventeenth century, mercantilism had been generally accepted as an economic theory. Seeking a favorable balance of trade, Englishmen saw two ways in which overseas possessions, or colonies, might make their country prosperous. The most direct way was to find gold and silver. The Spaniards had done that, and Englishmen hoped they could do the same. The second way was to obtain products from the colony that otherwise would have to be bought from foreign nations.

There was another reason why thoughtful Englishmen were interested in colonies. An increase in sheep raising caused a rise in the number of unemployed agricultural workers. It was believed that these men could be recruited by colonizing companies and sent to the colonies.

Such were the reasons that made the rulers of England, the nobles, and the merchants interested in founding colonies. But the motives of the emigrants for settling in the colonies were different. In the sixteenth century, when the Anglican Church had been established, all Englishmen had to worship according to the Anglican beliefs. Catholics, and other Protestants, called Separatists, were denied freedom of worship. Many Separatists, and particularly the Pilgrims, believing in discarding all of the outward aspects of Catholicism such as rituals and bishops, sought religious freedom in the new colonies. English Quakers, Presbyterians, Baptists, Catholics, Jews, and French Huguenots followed the earlier colonists into the North American settlements or founded their own.

In addition, because of the war between Holland and Spain, the English export wool trade was disrupted. This falloff in trade, plus the general overpopulation, led many farmers and artisans to hope that in a colony they could make a better living than at home.

4. The principal idea of the fourth paragraph is:

_____

_____

_____

Answer: Many farmers and artisans hoped that they could make a better living in the colonies than at home.

5. Which of these is the best statement of the principal idea of the *entire selection?*
   a. The chief results of establishing colonies for the English merchant class of the seventeenth century were a favorable balance of trade and religious freedom.
   b. The motives of the emigrants settling in the colonies were quite different from the motives of the rulers and merchant class who established them.
   c. The English of the seventeenth century saw the advantages of colonies: first of all, as a source of gold and silver; secondly, as a source of cheap products.
   d. The most important reasons for establishing colonies in seventeenth-century England were religious freedom, a favorable balance of trade, and additional opportunities to raise the standard of living for the working class and the unemployed.

Answer: *d.*

AFRICA SOUTH OF THE SAHARA

Because Africa south of the Sahara has never been a center of widespread world civilization, it used to be regarded as less important than Europe or the Islamic world, both of which have had a period of world leadership. Principally for this reason, historians once thought of world history as limited to the areas of more complex civilization. Recently, they have begun to realize that Africa is far more important than they previously thought. As African states have gained their independence and a subsequent voice in world affairs, their importance has increased. Today's historians recognize that a full understanding of human society must include all societies and not be restricted to a study of the most favored parts of the world.

It has already been explained earlier in this book that civilization advanced most rapidly where populations were relatively dense, and where there was some sort of communication between peoples so that one society could make contact with other societies through trade and the exchange of ideas. Until the birth of Christ, northern Europe and Africa south of the Sahara were on the fringes of civilization—outside the great "belt" of intercommunication stretching from the eastern Mediterranean to China. The expansion of the Roman Empire brought northern Europe into closer contact with world civilization, and the fifteenth-century development of sea-based commerce made Europe the center of a worldwide network of intercommunication. Africa, meanwhile, cut off by the Sahara and other physical barriers, could not participate fully in this expansion. It was not until the early part of the twentieth century that Africa came completely within the area of intercommunication.

The growth and development of African civilization in the face of these disadvantages is a part of the total human experience. Achievements accomplished under hardship are often as important to an understanding of history as those won more easily. The history of Africa can be regarded as one example of triumph over odds.

In world history, it is important to understand how the entire modern world arrived at its present stage. In addition, for Americans, African history has a special importance. More of our own ancestors came from Africa south of the Sahara than from any other part of the world except Europe. The history of the Western Hemisphere, then, owes much to African culture, and its study will reveal some of the rich origins of the Negro-American heritage.

1. The principal idea of the first paragraph is:
   a. A full understanding of human society must include all societies and not be restricted to a study of the most favored parts of the world.
   b. Africa south of the Sahara has never been a center of widespread world civilization.
   c. Africa is far more important than previously thought: as African states have gained their independence and a subsequent voice in world affairs, their importance has increased.
   d. Historians in the past have concentrated their studies on Europe and the Islamic world.

Answer: c.

2. Complete this statement of the principal idea in paragraph 2:
   Africa was cut off from the worldwide network of intercommunication by

Answer: the Sahara and other physical boundaries.

3. The principal idea of paragraph 3 is:

Answer: The history of Africa can be regarded as one example of triumph over odds.

AFRICA SOUTH OF THE SAHARA

Because Africa south of the Sahara has never been a center of widespread world civilization, it used to be regarded as less important than Europe or the Islamic world, both of which have had a period of world leadership. Principally for this reason, historians once thought of world history as limited to the areas of more complex civilization. Recently, they have begun to realize that Africa is far more important than they previously thought. As African states have gained their independence and a subsequent voice in world affairs, their importance has increased. Today's historians recognize that a full understanding of human society must include all societies and not be restricted to a study of the most favored parts of the world.

It has already been explained earlier in this book that civilization advanced most rapidly where populations were relatively dense, and where there was some sort of communication between peoples so that one society could make contact with other societies through trade and the exchange of ideas. Until the birth of Christ, northern Europe and Africa south of the Sahara were on the fringes of civilization—outside the great "belt" of intercommunication stretching from the eastern Mediterranean to China. The expansion of the Roman Empire brought northern Europe into closer contact with world civilization, and the fifteenth-century development of sea-based commerce made Europe the center of a worldwide network of intercommunication. Africa, meanwhile, cut off by the Sahara and other physical barriers, could not participate fully in this expansion. It was not until the early part of the twentieth century that Africa came completely within the area of intercommunication.

The growth and development of African civilization in the face of these disadvantages is a part of the total human experience. Achievements accomplished under hardship are often as important to an understanding of history as those won more easily. The history of Africa can be regarded as one example of triumph over odds.

In world history, it is important to understand how the entire modern world arrived at its present stage. In addition, for Americans, African history has a special importance. More of our own ancestors came from Africa south of the Sahara than from any other part of the world except Europe. The history of the Western Hemisphere, then, owes much to African culture, and its study will reveal some of the rich origins of the Negro-American heritage.

4. The principal idea of paragraph 4 is:

_____

_____

_____

Answer: The history of the Western Hemisphere owes much to African culture since more of our ancestors came from Africa south of the Sahara than from any other part of the world except Europe.

TRANSFORMATION OF TROPICAL AFRICA

In many ways, the transformation of tropical Africa during the first 1,000 years after Christ was an amazing feat. The barrier of the Sahara was partly overcome by the use of camels. The earlier failure to pass from the New Stone Age to the Bronze Age as rapidly as did the Mediterranean peoples was partly countered by the rapid spread of iron technology. The Moslem religion and literacy in Arabic were beginning to spread and would become more prevalent during the next 500 years. But then tropical African progress began to falter. The sixteenth and seventeenth centuries were a time of troubles in many regions of the continent.

Both Western and Moslem civilization passed a kind of turning point about 1500. Much the same thing happened in tropical Africa, and the change was partly associated with the changes in the technically more advanced civilizations to the north. Firearms made possible everywhere the concentration of power in the hands of a few. On land, use of these weapons was one reason for the rise of the three Moslem empires in the sixteenth and seventeenth centuries. At sea, the Portuguese could challenge Asians in the Indian Ocean.

Even without the use of artillery, the great maritime advances of the fifteenth-century Portuguese changed the direction of African trade. European ships could now appear on any coast of Africa. South of the equatorial forest, the Portuguese provided the first direct contact with the outside world for the more isolated societies. The speed and efficiency of the Bantu migration into central and southern Africa had tended to cut these people off from the later developments in the western Sudan. Now their isolation was again ended. Unfortunately, they were poorly prepared to cope with the Europeans, who had profited from the technological progress of the past thousand years.

1. The principal idea of the first paragraph is:

   a. The transformation of tropical Africa during the first 1,000 years after Christ was an amazing feat.

   b. Tropical Africa was transformed during the first 1,000 years after Christ as a result of the use of camels, the rapid spread of iron technology, and of Moslem religion and literacy in Arabic.

   c. The barrier of the Sahara was partly overcome by the use of camels.

   d. The sixteenth and seventeenth centuries were a time of troubles in many regions of the continent.

Answer: *b.*

2. Complete this statement of the principal idea of the second paragraph: Africa passed a kind of turning point about 1500 partly because of the changes in the _____

Answer: technically more advanced civilizations to the north.

3. The principal idea of the third paragraph is:

_____

_____

_____

Answer: Even without the use of artillery, the maritime advances of the fifteenth-century Portuguese changed Africa by providing contact with the outside world.

Part 2
Understanding
Details

Now that you are able to recognize the principal idea in scientific passages, we can turn our attention to understanding how the other sentences in a paragraph support or expand upon the principal idea.

These supporting sentences contain *details* which usually fall in one of four broad categories:

1. Sometimes details *define*. Often in scientific writing new terms will be introduced and defined for you.
2. Sometimes details *explain*. The principal idea is often a general concept which is further expanded upon by explanatory details.
3. Sometimes details *illustrate*. In this category we would place *examples* which are perhaps the most common of all types of details.
4. Sometimes details *compare*. This last category includes details which expand upon the principal idea by comparing or contrasting concepts or objects.

In the exercises that follow, all four categories are represented. Sometimes you will be asked to try *not* to refer to the passage when answering certain questions. This is to test your comprehension of the details. However, because this is a *self*-testing technique, for your benefit only, if you find you can't answer a question, by all means refer to the passage to refresh your memory.

Some of the passages will be repeated from the first section. You will again be asked to find the principal idea; however, now you will also see how the details support that idea.

Turn the page and read the passage on "Life Processes." Then do the exercises that follow it.

LIFE PROCESSES

Life processes, or those processes performed by all living forms in order to maintain life, are grouped under the general heading of *metabolism*. In a very broad sense, the energy relations that result in the utilization of food, and in the promotion of growth, are considered to be building-up processes and are often referred to as *anabolism*. *Catabolism*, on the other hand, is taken to mean the breakdown of stored reserves, which leaves the organism with a reduced store of energy. Very often it is difficult to classify some reactions accurately under these headings. For example, is the breakdown of a food substance into simpler substances, so that these, in turn, can be converted into fat and stored, an example of anabolism, catabolism, or both?

SOMETIMES DETAILS DEFINE

The principal idea of this passage is:

  a. Life processes are those processes performed by all living forms in order to maintain life.
  b. Energy relations that result in the utilization of growth are considered to be building-up processes or anabolism.
  c. Catabolism and anabolism are two processes performed by all living forms in order to maintain life and are grouped under the general heading of metabolism.
  d. Catabolism leaves the organism with a reduced store of energy.

Answer: *c.*

The details which support or expand upon the principal idea are, in this case, *definitions*. In this paragraph three important terms are defined: metabolism, anabolism, and catabolism. The author has italicized them to alert you to their importance. The principal idea (*c* above) states only *generally* that the paragraph is about these three processes.

We can say, then, that the three important details of this paragraph are:

  1. The definition of metabolism.
  2. The definition of anabolism.
  3. The definition of catabolism.

The last two sentences in the paragraph pose a question drawn from these details.

Now read the paragraph again, carefully; then try to answer the following questions without referring to the passage.

1. Catabolism is:

  a. Energy relations that result in the utilization of food and in the promotion of growth.
  b. The breakdown of stored reserves, leaving the organism with a reduced store of energy.
  c. The general heading for processes performed by all living forms in order to maintain life.

Answer: *b.*

LIFE PROCESSES

Life processes, or those processes performed by all living forms in order to maintain life, are grouped under the general heading of *metabolism*. In a very broad sense, the energy relations that result in the utilization of food, and in the promotion of growth, are considered to be building-up processes and are often referred to as *anabolism*. *Catabolism*, on the other hand, is taken to mean the breakdown of stored reserves, which leaves the organism with a reduced store of energy. Very often it is difficult to classify some reactions accurately under these headings. For example, is the breakdown of a food substance into simpler substances, so that these, in turn, can be converted into fat and stored, an example of anabolism, catabolism, or both?

2. Anabolism is:
   a. Energy relations that result in the utilization of food and in the pro-
      motion of growth.
   b. The breakdown of stored reserves, leaving the organism with a re-
      duced store of energy.
   c. The general heading for processes performed by all living forms in
      order to maintain life.

Answer: *a.*

3. Metabolism is:
   a. Energy relations that result in the utilization of food and in the pro-
      motion of growth.
   b. The breakdown of stored reserves, leaving the organism with a re-
      duced store of energy.
   c. The general heading for processes performed by all living forms in
      order to maintain life.

Answer: *c.*

FOOD HABITS

Feeding Animals differ widely in their food habits. Some insects feed on the tissues or juices of a single species of plant or the blood of one kind of animal, but most animals take several or many kinds of food. Cattle, deer, rodents, and insects that eat leaves and stems of plants are said to be *herbivorous;* cats, sharks, flesh flies, and many marine animals whose food is entirely or largely of other animals are termed *carnivorous;* and man, bears, rats, and others that eat various plant and animal materials are called general feeders, or *omnivorous.*

Paramecium, some sea anemones, and certain fishes that feed on small particles, living or dead, such as plankton, are termed microphagous feeders. In contrast, most higher animals, including man, that use larger materials are macrophagous feeders. Still other animals are fluid feeders, like the mosquitoes that suck blood and the aphids that pump in plant juices.

SOMETIMES DETAILS DEFINE

1. The principal idea of the first paragraph is:
   a. Animals differ widely in their food habits.
   b. Most animals take several or many kinds of food.
   c. Animals that eat various plant and animal materials are called general feeders, or omnivores.
   d. Animals differ widely in their food habits: they can be herbivorous, carnivorous, or omnivorous.

Answer: *d.*

2. The three important details in this paragraph are the definitions of:
   _____ , _____ , and _____

Answer: herbivorous, carnivorous, omnivorous.

3. Match the following (try *not* to refer to the passage):
   a. Herbivorous   _____ Animals that eat various plant and animal materials.
   b. Carnivorous   _____ Animals that eat leaves and stems of plants.
   c. Omnivorous   _____ Animals whose food is entirely or largely of other animals.

Answer: *c, a, b.*

4. The principal idea of the second paragraph is:
   a. Animals are classified as microphagous, macrophagous, or fluid feeders according to the size and type of food they eat.
   b. Most higher animals are macrophagous feeders.
   c. Fluid feeders suck the blood of other animals or pump in the juices of plants.
   d. There are three different classifications of animal feeders.

Answer: *a.*

FOOD HABITS

Feeding Animals differ widely in their food habits. Some insects feed on the tissues or juices of a single species of plant or the blood of one kind of animal, but most animals take several or many kinds of food. Cattle, deer, rodents, and insects that eat leaves and stems of plants are said to be *herbivorous;* cats, sharks, flesh flies, and many marine animals whose food is entirely or largely of other animals are termed *carnivorous;* and man, bears, rats, and others that eat various plant and animal materials are called general feeders, or *omnivorous.*

Paramecium, some sea anemones, and certain fishes that feed on small particles, living or dead, such as plankton, are termed microphagous feeders. In contrast, most higher animals, including man, that use larger materials are macrophagous feeders. Still other animals are fluid feeders, like the mosquitoes that suck blood and the aphids that pump in plant juices.

5. The three important details of the second paragraph are the definitions of _____ , _____ , and _____ feeders.

Answer: microphagous, macrophagous, and fluid

6. Match the following (try *not* to refer to the passage):
   a. Microphagous   _____ Animals that suck the blood of other animals or pump in the juices of plants.
   b. Macrophagous   _____ Animals that feed on small particles, living or dead.
   c. Fluid feeders   _____ Higher animals, including man, that eat large materials (animal and plant).

Answer: *c, a, b.*

THE SEASONS

The year of the seasons   The year is the period of the earth's revolution, or of the sun's apparent motion in the ecliptic. The kind of year depends on the point in the sky to which the sun's motion is referred, whether this point is fixed or is itself in motion. Just as the day in common use is not the true period of the earth's rotation, so the year of the seasons is not the true period of its revolution. Two kinds of year have the greatest use.

The *sidereal year* is the interval of time in which the sun apparently performs a complete revolution with reference to a fixed point on the celestial sphere. Its length is 365^d 6^h 9^m 10^s ($365^d.25636$) of mean solar time, which is now increasing at the rate of $0^s.01$ a century, in addition to any change caused by variations in the rate of the earth's rotation. The sidereal year is the true period of the earth's revolution.

The *tropical year* is the interval between two successive returns of the sun to the vernal equinox. Its length is 365^d 5^h 48^m 46^s ($365^d.24220$) of mean solar time and is now diminishing at the rate of $0^s.53$ a century. It is the year of the seasons, the year to which the calendar conforms as nearly as possible. Because of the westward precession of the equinox, the sun returns to the equinox before it has gone completely around the ecliptic. The year of the seasons is shorter than the sidereal year by the fraction $50''.26/360°$ of 365.25636 days, or a little more than 20 minutes.

SOMETIMES DETAILS DEFINE

1. The principal idea of the *entire passage* is:
   a. The year of the seasons is shorter than the sidereal year by a little more than twenty minutes.
   b. The year is the period of the earth's revolution.
   c. Two kinds of year have the greatest use: the sidereal year and the tropical year.
   d. The tropical year is the interval between two successive returns of the sun to the vernal equinox.

Answer: *c.*

2. In the first paragraph the word ＿＿＿＿＿＿ is defined.

Answer: year

3. In the second paragraph the term ＿＿＿＿＿＿＿ is defined.

Answer: sidereal year

4. In the third paragraph, the term ＿＿＿＿＿＿＿ is defined.

Answer: tropical year

THE SEASONS

The year of the seasons   The year is the period of the earth's revolution, or of the sun's apparent motion in the ecliptic. The kind of year depends on the point in the sky to which the sun's motion is referred, whether this point is fixed or is itself in motion. Just as the day in common use is not the true period of the earth's rotation, so the year of the seasons is not the true period of its revolution. Two kinds of year have the greatest use.

The *sidereal year* is the interval of time in which the sun apparently performs a complete revolution with reference to a fixed point on the celestial sphere. Its length is 365^d 6^h 9^m 10^s ($365^d.25636$) of mean solar time, which is now increasing at the rate of $0^s.01$ a century, in addition to any change caused by variations in the rate of the earth's rotation. The sidereal year is the true period of the earth's revolution.

The *tropical year* is the interval between two successive returns of the sun to the vernal equinox. Its length is 365^d 5^h 48^m 46^s ($365^d.24220$) of mean solar time and is now diminishing at the rate of $0^s.53$ a century. It is the year of the seasons, the year to which the calendar conforms as nearly as possible. Because of the westward precession of the equinox, the sun returns to the equinox before it has gone completely around the ecliptic. The year of the seasons is shorter than the sidereal year by the fraction $50''.26/360°$ of 365.25636 days, or a little more than 20 minutes.

5. Match the following (try *not* to refer to the passage):

a. Year   _____ The period of the earth's revolution or of the sun's apparent motion in the ecliptic.

b. Sidereal year   _____ The interval between two successive returns of the sun to the vernal equinox.

c. Tropical year   _____ The interval of time in which the sun apparently performs a complete revolution with reference to a fixed point on the celestial sphere.

Answer: *a, c, b.*

MODIFICATIONS OF FREUD'S THEORY

From the time of Freud's formulation of this theory until the present, many psychiatrists have continued to subscribe to it in its original form. Other psychiatrists and psychologists have modified it in accordance with their own observations and experience. The first important modifications came around 1912 when both Carl Jung and Alfred Adler differed with Freud and left his inner circle of students. Both Adler and Jung disagreed with Freud's great emphasis on sex motivation as the central one in human behavior. Adler stressed the drive for power and mastery and made this "superiority" motive central in human behavior in place of Freud's sex instinct. Jung emphasized the development of a meaningful relationship between the conscious and the unconscious. Symbols were, to him, important conscious representatives of unconscious processes. Hence, he believed that symbols supply each person with a key to his unconscious. Jung found rich sources of symbolism in many areas of study such as archeology, art, history, alchemy, and religion. Since he had a very extensive background in the study of religion, Jung made frequent use of religious symbols in his analytical psychology.

SOMETIMES DETAILS EXPLAIN

The principal idea of this paragraph is:

a. Many psychiatrists still subscribe to Freud's theory in its original form.
b. Some psychiatrists and psychologists have modified Freud's original theory; both Carl Jung and Alfred Adler disagreed with Freud's emphasis on sex motivation as the central one in human behavior.
c. Carl Jung emphasized the development of a meaningful relationship between the conscious and the unconscious.
d. The first important modifications of Freud's theory came around 1912.

Answer: *b*.

Read the principal idea (*b*. above) carefully. We would expect the supporting details in this passage to *explain* how Jung and Adler differed from Freud.

Read the paragraph again, and then try to answer the following questions about the supporting details (try *not* to refer to the passage):

1. In place of Freud's emphasis on the sex instinct, Adler thought the central motive in human behavior was:
   a. Religious symbols.
   b. The drive for power and mastery.
   c. The unconscious mind.

Answer: *b*.

2. Carl Jung also disagreed with Freud. However, Jung emphasized a meaningful relationship between:
   a. Sex and art.
   b. Motivation and sex.
   c. The conscious and the unconscious.

Answer: *c*.

MODIFICATIONS OF FREUD'S THEORY

From the time of Freud's formulation of this theory until the present, many psychiatrists have continued to subscribe to it in its original form. Other psychiatrists and psychologists have modified it in accordance with their own observations and experience. The first important modifications came around 1912 when both Carl Jung and Alfred Adler differed with Freud and left his inner circle of students. Both Adler and Jung disagreed with Freud's great emphasis on sex motivation as the central one in human behavior. Adler stressed the drive for power and mastery and made this "superiority" motive central in human behavior in place of Freud's sex instinct. Jung emphasized the development of a meaningful relationship between the conscious and the unconscious. Symbols were, to him, important conscious representatives of unconscious processes. Hence, he believed that symbols supply each person with a key to his unconscious. Jung found rich sources of symbolism in many areas of study such as archeology, art, history, alchemy, and religion. Since he had a very extensive background in the study of religion, Jung made frequent use of religious symbols in his analytical psychology.

3. To Jung, the important conscious representatives of unconscious processes were:
   a.   Religion.
   b.   Motives.
   c.   Symbols.

Answer: *c.*

ORIGIN OF PETROLEUM

The manner of origin of petroleum is still not completely understood, but geologists agree that it formed from animals and plants which lived in the sea at the time the sediments were being deposited. The evidence for this origin is overwhelming. First, petroleum is related to organic matter chemically and in its optical properties. Second, all extensive occurrences of petroleum are associated with sedimentary rocks. Third, large amounts of petroleum are never found except in association with rocks with numerous marine fossils.

As the sediments were deposited, oil was formed by partial decay of animal and plant tissue and was buried in the accumulating sediment. This organic material remained in the sediment as it was altered to rock. Dark shales are likely to be highly bituminous and oil can be extracted from them, but the present cost is uneconomic. The petroleum in most cases has moved out of the original sediment and has entered porous layers. In these porous layers, it moved upward and accumulated in traps, i.e., in places where impervious material prevented further movement.

SOMETIMES DETAILS EXPLAIN

Sometimes the details in a passage support or expand upon the principal idea by explaining it more fully or by clarifying it with additional facts.

In the passage "Origin of Petroleum" the details help to *explain* the scientific principle.

First let's find the principal idea of the passage. It is:

a. Petroleum is related to organic matter chemically and in its optical properties.

b. The manner of origin of petroleum is not completely known, but it is formed from animals and plants which lived in the sea at the time sediments were deposited.

c. All extensive occurrences of petroleum are associated with sedimentary rocks.

d. Large amounts of petroleum are never found except in association with rocks with numerous marine fossils.

Answer: *b.*

The three important explanatory details in the paragraph are easy to spot because the author uses the words "First," "Second," and "Third" to introduce each one.

Read the principal idea (*b.* above) again; then answer the following questions about the supporting details without referring to the passage.

1. Petroleum is related to _____ chemically and in its optical properties.

a. Inorganic matter.

b. Sediment.

c. Organic matter.

Answer: *c.*

ORIGIN OF PETROLEUM

The manner of origin of petroleum is still not completely understood, but geologists agree that it formed from animals and plants which lived in the sea at the time the sediments were being deposited. The evidence for this origin is overwhelming. First, petroleum is related to organic matter chemically and in its optical properties. Second, all extensive occurrences of petroleum are associated with sedimentary rocks. Third, large amounts of petroleum are never found except in association with rocks with numerous marine fossils.

As the sediments were deposited, oil was formed by partial decay of animal and plant tissue and was buried in the accumulating sediment. This organic material remained in the sediment as it was altered to rock. Dark shales are likely to be highly bituminous and oil can be extracted from them, but the present cost is uneconomic. The petroleum in most cases has moved out of the original sediment and has entered porous layers. In these porous layers, it moved upward and accumulated in traps, i.e., in places where impervious material prevented further movement.

2. All extensive occurrences of petroleum are associated with _____

   a. The ocean.
   b. Sedimentary rocks.
   c. Plant life.

Answer: *b.*

3. Large amounts of _____ are never found except in association with rocks with numerous marine fossils.
   a. Petroleum.
   b. Sediment.
   c. Plants.

Answer: *a.*

PROTEIN SENSITIVITY

As a result of their complicated geometric makeup, proteins are extremely sensitive to chemical and physical influences. Excessive heat, pressure, electricity, heavy metals, and many other agents produce protein **denaturation:** cross-linkages within the folded amino acid chain are broken, the exquisite geometry of arrangement is disarranged or destroyed, and the molecule collapses. Extreme disarrangement is spoken of as **coagulation.** In living matter, a protein in a slightly denatured state may sometimes revert to the native state, and vice versa. But once coagulated, like boiled egg white, a protein usually cannot be restored to its native form. Cellular death is sometimes a result of irreversible protein coagulation.

SOMETIMES DETAILS EXPLAIN

First let's find the principal idea of this paragraph, and then we'll see how the details expand upon it.

The principal idea is:
  a. Proteins have a complex geometric makeup.
  b. In living matter, a protein in a slightly denatured state may some-times revert to the natural state.
  c. Due to its complex geometric structure, protein is extremely sensitive to chemical and physical influences.
  d. Proteins can be compared to boiled egg whites.

Answer: c.

Read the principal idea (c. above) again. We would expect the supporting details in this case to explain what happens when protein is exposed to physical and chemical influence.

Read the entire paragraph again, and then try to answer the following questions without referring to it.

1. Excessive heat, pressure, electricity, heavy metals, and many other agents produce protein _____
  a. Destruction.
  b. Denaturation.
  c. Expansion.

Answer: b.

2. Protein denaturation causes cross-linkages within the folded amino acid chain to be _____
  a. Joined.
  b. Stretched.
  c. Broken.

Answer: c.

PROTEIN SENSITIVITY

As a result of their complicated geometric makeup, proteins are extremely sensitive to chemical and physical influences. Excessive heat, pressure, electricity, heavy metals, and many other agents produce protein **denaturation:** cross-linkages within the folded amino acid chain are broken, the exquisite geometry of arrangement is disarranged or destroyed, and the molecule collapses. Extreme disarrangement is spoken of as **coagulation**. In living matter, a protein in a slightly denatured state may sometimes revert to the native state, and vice versa. But once coagulated, like boiled egg white, a protein usually cannot be restored to its native form. Cellular death is sometimes a result of irreversible protein coagulation.

3. Extreme disarrangement of the geometric makeup of proteins is called

_____

   a. Coagulation.
   b. Denaturation.
   c. Native.

Answer: *a.*

4. Cellular death is _____ a result of irreversible protein coagulation.
   a. Never.
   b. Sometimes.
   c. Always.

Answer: *b.*

ENERGY AND ITS CONSERVATION

Energy is defined as the ability or capacity to do work. It occurs in many forms. A swinging hammer can do work by virtue of its motion; energy associated with motion is known as *kinetic energy*. A raised pile driver can do work by virtue of its elevated position; it has what we call *potential energy*. When we buy gasoline, we buy chemical energy. The food we eat provides energy for our living. We purchase electrical energy so our electric motors can do work for us. Energy may exist in the form of electromagnetic radiation; indeed, the earth's primary source of energy lies in the radiation it receives from the sun. Much of physics involves the relationships among the many forms of energy and the transformations from one form to another.

SOMETIMES DETAILS ILLUSTRATE

Perhaps the most commonly used details are examples or illustrations.

1. In this passage on energy, the examples of kinds of energy illustrate the general scientific principle which is:
   a. Energy may exist in the form of electromagnetic radiation; indeed, the earth's primary source of energy lies in the radiation it receives from the sun.
   b. A swinging hammer can do work by virtue of its motion; energy associated with motion is known as kinetic energy.
   c. Energy, which occurs in many forms, is defined as the capacity to do work.
   d. A raised pile driver can do work by virtue of its elevated position; it has what we call potential energy.

Answer: c.

The passage gives six examples of kinds of energy. In the principal idea, energy is defined as "the ability or capacity to do work." Let's see how the examples support this idea.

2. All the following statements except *one* are examples which support the principal idea of this passage. Which one does not? (Try *not* to refer to the passage.)
   a. Energy associated with motion is known as kinetic energy.
   b. The food we eat provides energy for our living.
   c. Physics involves the relationships among the many forms of energy.
   d. We purchase electrical energy so our electric motors can do work for us.

Answer: c.

RESEMBLANCES AND DIFFERENCES IN ANIMALS

Methods and purposes   Various degrees of resemblance and difference are easily seen in any mixed assemblage of animals. Of the domestic animals on a farm, the cow and sheep both have horns and cloven hoofs but differ in size, shape, color, and body covering. A horse agrees with the cow and sheep in having long legs and teeth of the grinding type but lacks horns and has solid hoofs. A dog differs from all three in having nails and pads on its separate toes and having teeth of the stabbing and shearing types; it agrees in being covered with hair. The cat resembles the dog more closely than the hoofed animals. All these animals have hair and teeth, they produce living young, which they suckle, and they show many other features in common. As a group they all differ from the chickens and ducks, which are covered with feathers, lack teeth, and lay eggs—but these and all other birds have eyes, lungs, four limbs, and other characters like the four-footed animals named. So it is, by likenesses and differences, that animals may be divided into minor and major groups.

SOMETIMES DETAILS ILLUSTRATE

1. The principal idea of this paragraph is:
   a. It is by various degrees of resemblance and difference that animals may be divided into minor and major groups.
   b. Animals differ in size, shape, color, and body covering.
   c. Some farm animals have many features in common.
   d. The cat resembles the dog more closely than the hoofed animals.

Answer: *a.*

2. All the following statements except *one* are examples which support the principal idea of this paragraph by illustrating it. Which one is not? (Try *not* to refer to the passage.)
   a. Of the domestic animals on a farm, the cow and sheep both have horns and cloven hoofs but differ in size, shape, color, and body covering.
   b. Animals resemble each other and differ from each other in various degrees.
   c. The cat resembles the dog more closely than the hoofed animals.
   d. Ducks and all other birds have eyes, lungs, four limbs, and other characters like four-footed animals.

Answer: *b.*

AFTERIMAGES

When we look at a bright light and then close our eyes, we see a fleeting bright spot and then a lingering dark one. In this case we have experienced a *positive* and a *negative afterimage*. These afterimages occur because the retina continues to respond for a time after the cessation of the stimulus. This phenomenon allows us to see motion when a series of still photographs are projected rapidly on a movie screen in the proper sequence. Afterimages also occur with colored stimuli. In these cases the positive afterimage is the same hue as the stimulus and the negative one is the complementary hue. For example, if we stare at a blue light and then close our eyes, we will see a momentary blue spot and then a persisting yellow one.

The study of afterimages emphasizes again the psychological nature of perception. The motion in a motion picture is psychological, not physical; it is a matter of the interpretation in the central nervous system of a series of still photographs. The yellow negative afterimage that comes after looking at a blue light is also a central phenomenon, for no "yellow" stimulus exists in the environment. A study of only physical stimuli will never reveal what a person senses and perceives. Only a study of the actual behavior of the organism will give us information about the perceived world.

SOMETIMES DETAILS ILLUSTRATE

1. The principal idea of the first paragraph is:
    a.   Afterimages occur with colored stimuli.
    b.   When we look at a bright light and then close our eyes, we see a fleet-
        ing bright spot and then a lingering dark one.
    c.   There are both positive and negative afterimages.
    d.   Positive and negative afterimages occur because the retina continues
        to respond for a time after the cessation of the stimulus.

Answer: *d.*

2. The principal idea of this passage is illustrated by three details. Which
    one of the following statements is *not* an illustration of the idea (try *not*
    to refer to the passage):
    a.   We see motion when a series of still photographs is projected on a
        screen in the proper sequence.
    b.   The pupils of our eyes expand when we enter a dark movie theater.
    c.   When we look at a bright light and then close our eyes, we see a fleet-
        ing bright spot and then a lingering dark one.
    d.   If we stare at a blue light and then close our eyes, we will see a mo-
        mentary blue spot and then a persisting yellow one.

Answer: *b.*

SCIENCE IS A LANGUAGE

Fundamentally, science is a *language,* a system of communication comparable to the systems of religion, art, politics, English, or French. Like the latter, science enables man to travel in new countries of the mind, and to understand and be understood in such countries. Like other languages, moreover, science has its grammar—the methods of scientific inquiry; its authors and its literature—the scientists and their written work; and its various dialects or forms of expression—physics, chemistry, and biology, for example.

SOMETIMES DETAILS COMPARE

Sometimes, in order to make his point clearer, an author will *compare* his subject with another, more familiar, concept.

1. In the accompanying passage, science is compared to a _____

Answer: language.

The details in this paragraph all contribute to the comparison. Let's see how they all relate to the principal idea.

2. The principal idea of this paragraph is:
   a. Science has many forms of expression.
   b. Science is a language, a system of communication comparable to the systems of religion, art, politics, English, or French.
   c. Science has its authors and its literature—the scientists and their written work.
   d. Science enables man to travel in new countries of the mind.

Answer: *b.*

We would expect the details in this comparison to show in what ways science is like a language.

3. Which of the following statements is *not* part of the comparison between science and language? (Try *not* to refer to the passage.)
   a. Like a language, science enables man to understand or be understood in other countries.
   b. Science has its grammar—the methods of scientific inquiry.
   c. Science has its various dialects or forms of expression—physics, chemistry, and biology, for example.
   d. Different systems of religion, politics, etc., have their own dialects or forms of expression.

Answer: *d.*

NUTRITION

One of the principal activities of living organisms is *nutrition*, a process which provides the raw materials for maintenance of life. All living matter has an unceasing requirement for such raw materials, for the very act of living continuously uses up two basic commodities: energy and matter. In this respect a living organism is like a mechanical engine or indeed like any other action-performing system in the universe. Energy is needed to power the system, to make the parts operate, to keep activity going—in short, to maintain function. And matter is needed to replace parts, to repair breakdowns, to continue the system intact and able to function—in short, to maintain structure. Therefore, by its very nature as an action-performing unit, a "living" organism can remain alive only if it continuously expends energy and matter. These commodities must be replenished from the outside at least as fast as they are used up inside, and the replenishment function is nutrition.

SOMETIMES DETAILS COMPARE

1. In the accompanying paragraph, what two things are compared to each other? _____ and _____

Answer: A living organism and a mechanical engine.

2. The principal idea of this passage is:
   a. One of the principal activities of living organisms is nutrition.
   b. Like a mechanical engine, a living organism has an unceasing requirement for raw materials and continuously uses up two basic commodities: energy and matter.
   c. A "living" organism can remain alive only if it continuously expends energy and matter.
   d. Energy is needed to power any system, to make the parts operate, to keep activity going—in short, to maintain structure.

Answer: b.

3. Which of the following statements does not contribute to the comparison between a living organism and a mechanical machine? (Try not to refer to the passage.)
   a. Energy is needed to power both in order to maintain function.
   b. Matter is needed by both to replace parts, to repair breakdowns, to continue the system intact and able to function—in short, to maintain structure.
   c. The process which provides raw material for maintenance of life is nutrition.
   d. Living organisms and mechanical engines are both action-performing systems.

Answer: c.

COMBINATIONS

In most written passages, more than one kind of detail is used. Authors often use examples to illustrate their points; at the same time they may use comparisons, explanations, and definitions—all within the same paragraph.

In the next three passages, you will decide what kinds of details (examples, comparisons, explanations, or definitions) the author is using. First, as before, you will find the principal idea. Then it will be clearer just how the details support or expand upon that idea.

WHO ARE THE POOR?

Poverty does not lend itself to precise definition. But as a broad generalization, we might say that a family lives in poverty when its basic needs exceed its available means of satisfying them. A family's needs have many determinants: its size, its health, the ages of its members, and so forth. Its means include currently earned income, transfer payments, past savings, and so on. The definition of poverty more or less officially accepted by concerned government agencies is that any family which receives from all sources an income less than $3,000 per year, or any unattached individual who receives less than $1,500 per year, is poor. Applying this definition to income data for the United States, it is found that *nearly one-fifth of the nation lives in poverty.*

1. The principal idea of this paragraph is:
   a. A family's needs have many determinants: its size, its health, the ages of its members, etc.
   b. Nearly one-fifth of the nation lives in poverty.
   c. A family lives in poverty when its basic needs exceed its available means of satisfying them.
   d. Poverty does not lend itself to precise definition.

Answer: *c.*

2. The details in this paragraph (choose two):
   a. Define poverty.
   b. Compare a small family to a small income.
   c. Explain a family's needs and resources.
   d. Illustrate a particular poverty situation.

Answers: *a* and *c.*

Try *not* to refer to the passage to answer the questions below.

3. How many definitions of poverty are given?
   a. One.
   b. Two.
   c. Three.
   d. Four.

Answer: *b.*

4. What three determinants of a family's needs are given?

_____

_____

_____

Answer: A family's *size*, its *health*, and the *ages of its members.*

WHO ARE THE POOR?

Poverty does not lend itself to precise definition. But as a broad generalization, we might say that a family lives in poverty when its basic needs exceed its available means of satisfying them. A family's needs have many determinants: its size, its health, the ages of its members, and so forth. Its means include currently earned income, transfer payments, past savings, and so on. The definition of poverty more or less officially accepted by concerned government agencies is that any family which receives from all sources an income less than $3,000 per year, or any unattached individual who receives less than $1,500 per year, is poor. Applying this definition to income data for the United States, it is found that *nearly one-fifth of the nation lives in poverty.*

5. What three resources or means of a family are given?

_____

_____

_____

Answer: Currently earned income, transfer payments, and past savings.

6. What fraction of the people of the United States live in poverty?
   a. One-fourth.
   b. One-sixth.
   c. One-fifth.
   d. One-eighth.

Answer: c.

CONTIGUITY

The concept of association implies contiguity. That is to say, for two physical events to be connected, and hence for the corresponding processes in the brain to become associated, they must occur at approximately the same time and place. They must be contiguous, or paired, events. For this reason, contiguity has long been stated as a basic law governing the formation of associations.

What must be contiguous varies with different learning situations. In simple conditioning, as we shall see, it is the contiguity of two stimuli that is essential for learning. In this case, we speak of the pairing of stimuli. In other, somewhat more complex learning situations, it is the contiguity of a response and a reward or punishment that is important for learning. For example, we give a dog a bit of food when he performs a trick, or we slap a child's hand when he reaches for a lighted cigarette. In every case, it is the pairing of events—making them contiguous—that is essential in learning.

Read the accompanying passage carefully, and then answer the questions below. You may refer to the passage as often as you like.

1. The principal idea of the first paragraph is:
  a. Contiguity has long been stated as a basic law governing the formation of associations.
  b. Contiguous events are paired events.
  c. Sometimes two physical events occur approximately at the same time.
  d. The concept of association involves processes of the brain.

Answer: a.

2. The details in the first paragraph:
  a. Compare the concept of contiguity to the workings of the brain.
  b. Give particular examples of contiguity.
  c. Define and explain the concept of contiguity.

Answer: c.

3. The principal idea of the second paragraph is:
  a. What must be contiguous varies with different learning situations.
  b. In both simple and complex conditioning it is the pairing of events— making them contiguous—that is essential for learning.
  c. In simple conditioning, it is the contiguity of two stimuli that is essential for learning.
  d. Slapping a child's hand when he reaches for a cigarette is a kind of conditioning.

Answer: b.

CONTIGUITY

The concept of association implies contiguity. That is to say, for two physical events to be connected, and hence for the corresponding processes in the brain to become associated, they must occur at approximately the same time and place. They must be contiguous, or paired, events. For this reason, contiguity has long been stated as a basic law governing the formation of associations.

What must be contiguous varies with different learning situations. In simple conditioning, as we shall see, it is the contiguity of two stimuli that is essential for learning. In this case, we speak of the pairing of stimuli. In other, somewhat more complex learning situations, it is the contiguity of a response and a reward or punishment that is important for learning. For example, we give a dog a bit of food when he performs a trick, or we slap a child's hand when he reaches for a lighted cigarette. In every case, it is the pairing of events—making them contiguous—that is essential in learning.

4. The details in the second paragraph (choose two):
   a. Give examples of contiguous or paired events.
   b. Compare slapping a child's hand to rewarding a dog's tricks.
   c. Define contiguity.
   d. Explain how contiguity applies to both simple and complex conditioning.

Answers: *a* and *d*.

THE CONTENT OF CULTURE

Many sociologists have classified the content of culture into two large components, material culture and nonmaterial culture. One sociologist, in fact, has used this distinction as the basis for an impressive theory of cultural change. The concept of material culture is clear enough. But the concept of nonmaterial culture is not quite so clear, except in the sense that it is a residual category, including everything that is not material. "Everything that is not material," however, may include items of several fundamentally different kinds, and this tendency to obscure significant distinctions is a logical weakness of residual categories. We shall therefore adopt a threefold classification of the content of culture.

Our classification stems directly from the definition of culture as the complex whole that consists of everything we think and do and have as members of society. Thinking and doing and having are three of the most fundamental categories in the grammar of any language. They give us the three components of culture—ideas, norms, and things. The last of these is the material culture mentioned above. Ideas and norms are both nonmaterial culture, but we distinguish them because they perform different functions in society and operate in different ways. We thus have the major categories or headings under which we can later locate the detailed items that make up this large phenomenon. The basic table on which we shall build now looks like this:

CULTURE

(Thinking)	*(Doing)*	*(Having)*
IDEAS	NORMS	MATERIAL

Read the accompanying passage carefully, and then answer the questions below. You may refer to the passage as often as you like.

1. The principal idea of the first paragraph is:
   a. Many sociologists disagree on the meaning of nonmaterial culture.
   b. Nonmaterial culture is a residual category, including everything that is not material.
   c. Many sociologists have classified the content of culture into two large components, material culture and nonmaterial culture.
   d. A tendency to obscure significant distinctions is a logical weakness of residual categories.

Answer: c.

2. The details in the first paragraph:
   a. Explain why the concept of nonmaterial culture is unclear.
   b. Define culture.
   c. Compare nonmaterial culture to various obscure categories.
   d. Give examples of material culture.

Answer: a.

3. The principal idea of the second paragraph is:
   a. Both ideas and norms are nonmaterial culture, but we distinguish them because they perform different functions in society.
   b. Thinking and doing and having are three of the most fundamental categories in the grammar of any language.
   c. Culture is the complex whole of everything we think (ideas) and do (norms) and have (things).
   d. The three components of culture are ideas, norms, and things.

Answer: c.

THE CONTENT OF CULTURE

Many sociologists have classified the content of culture into two large components, material culture and nonmaterial culture. One sociologist, in fact, has used this distinction as the basis for an impressive theory of cultural change. The concept of material culture is clear enough. But the concept of nonmaterial culture is not quite so clear, except in the sense that it is a residual category, including everything that is not material. "Everything that is not material," however, may include items of several fundamentally different kinds, and this tendency to obscure significant distinctions is a logical weakness of residual categories. We shall therefore adopt a threefold classification of the content of culture.

Our classification stems directly from the definition of culture as the complex whole that consists of everything we think and do and have as members of society. Thinking and doing and having are three of the most fundamental categories in the grammar of any language. They give us the three components of culture—ideas, norms, and things. The last of these is the material culture mentioned above. Ideas and norms are both nonmaterial culture, but we distinguish them because they perform different functions in society and operate in different ways. We thus have the major categories or headings under which we can later locate the detailed items that make up this large phenomenon. The basic table on which we shall build now looks like this:

CULTURE

(Thinking)	(Doing)	(Having)
IDEAS	NORMS	MATERIAL

4. The details in the second paragraph:
   - *a.*   Compare ideas to norms.
   - *b.*   Define culture.
   - *c.*   Explain the concept of material culture.
   - *d.*   Give examples of material culture.

Answer: *b.*

Part 3
Understanding
Experiments

Experimentation is a fundamental part of science as it validates or proves true certain hypotheses or "hunches" which scientists have about phenomena. When reading scientific material, you will often come across descriptions of experiments, and it is important for you to be able to comprehend and follow these descriptions.

The author will almost always present an experiment in a straightforward, step-by-step manner. All that you have to do is follow the logical sequence of the steps and visualize the experiment in your mind as you read. Usually an illustration or diagram will accompany the description, and of course it is always a good idea to study the illustration and to read the caption beneath it.

The exercises in this section will help you take apart each experiment step by step so that you can better understand the *purpose* of the experiment—that is, what principal idea it is establishing.

As in other parts of the book, you may refer to the excerpted passage as often as necessary.

Now turn the page and begin with the passage on "Movement of Glaciers."

MOVEMENT OF GLACIERS

Rate of movement   Judged by most standards, all glaciers move slowly, and it has been only in comparatively recent times that movement has been recognized as one of their characteristics.

A young Swiss, Louis Agassiz, was the first to prove definitely the movement of glaciers. While a boy he noticed in some of the valleys of the Alps that the relationship of bodies of ice to landmarks on the sides was not constant. He drove stakes in the valley outside the ice and stakes in line with them on the ice, and found that with the lapse of time the relationship of the stakes changed; those on the ice moved downvalley while the others remained stationary. Agassiz was of an inquiring turn of mind and was not satisfied with finding out merely that the glacier moved. He also measured the rate of movement of the glaciers on which he worked and demonstrated that the middle of the ice moved faster than the sides (Fig. 3-1).

In the warm season, a forward movement of a few inches per day is, perhaps, average for the ice near the margin of a glacier, and a movement of a few feet per day is rapid. It is scarcely believable that with such slow movements a glacier can be a powerful agent of transportation and mechanical weathering.

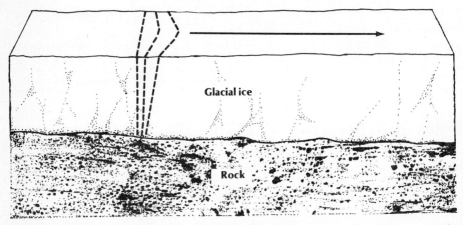

Fig. 3-1   Diagram showing differential movement within a valley glacier. Stakes driven in a straight line across the top of a glacier in a short time show a curve down-valley. Pegs placed on the side of the glacier demonstrate that the top moves faster than the bottom.

Read the experiment carefully. Then answer the questions below. You may refer to the passage as often as you like.

1. What did Louis Agassiz prove in his experiment?

_____

Answer (your own words): That glaciers move.

2. Below are the steps involved in Agassiz's experiment. You are to arrange them in their logical order of occurrence. (You may refer to the passage as often as you like.)

_____ Agassiz noted the relationship of distance between the stakes to the passage of time.

_____ As a boy in the Swiss Alps, Agassiz noticed that the relationship of bodies of ice to landmarks on the sides was not constant.

_____ He found that the stakes on the ice moved downvalley, while the others remained stationary.

_____ He drove stakes in the ice in line with those in the valley outside.

_____ He drove stakes in the valley outside the ice.

_____ He then measured the rate of movement and found that the middle of the ice moved faster than the sides.

Answers: 4, 1, 5, 3, 2, 6.

OXIDATION OF TIN

Lavoisier knew that tin could be converted to a white powder when it was heated, and the powder definitely weighed more than the original metal. To study the change in greater detail, Lavoisier placed a piece of tin on a wooden block floating in water (Fig. 3-2), covered the block with a glass jar, and heated the tin by focusing the sun's rays upon it with a magnifying glass—a common method of heating before gas burners and electric heaters were invented. The tin was partly changed to white powder, and the water level rose in the jar until only four-fifths as much air was left as there had been at the start. Further heating caused no detectable change. In another experiment Lavoisier heated tin in a sealed flask until as much as possible was converted to powder. The flask was weighed accurately before and after heating, and the two weights proved to be identical. Then the flask was opened, and air rushed in. With the additional air, the weight of the flask was greater than it had been at the start—and by the same amount as the increase in weight of the tin.

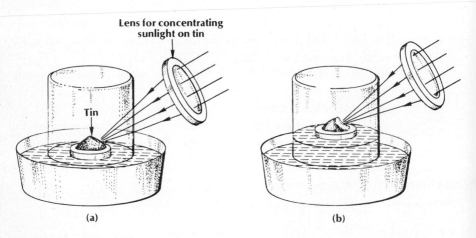

Fig. 3-2 Lavoisier's experiment showing that tin upon heating combines with a gas from the air: (a) Before heating; (b) after heating. The tin is partly changed to a white powder, and the water level rises until only four-fifths as much air is left as there was at the start. Further heating causes no additional change.

Read the accompanying passage carefully, and then answer the questions below. You may refer to the passage as often as you like.

1. How many experiments are described in this paragraph? _____

Answer: two.

2. The experiments were conducted by a man named _____

Answer: Lavoisier.

3. Both experiments were concerned with the conversion of tin to a _____

Answer: white powder.

4. Lavoisier wanted to find out why the white powder weighed more than the _____

Answer: tin (original metal).

5. Arrange the steps of the first experiment in the numerical order of their occurrence. You may refer to the passage if necessary.
   _____ Lavoisier heated the tin by focusing the sun's rays upon it with a magnifying glass.
   _____ He placed a piece of tin on a wooden block floating in water and covered the block with a glass jar.
   _____ Further heating caused no detectable change.
   _____ The tin was partly changed to white powder.
   _____ The water level rose in the jar until only four-fifths as much air was left as there had been at the start.

Answers: 2, 1, 5, 3, 4.

OXIDATION OF TIN

Lavoisier knew that tin could be converted to a white powder when it was heated, and the powder definitely weighed more than the original metal. To study the change in greater detail, Lavoisier placed a piece of tin on a wooden block floating in water (Fig. 3-2), covered the block with a glass jar, and heated the tin by focusing the sun's rays upon it with a magnifying glass—a common method of heating before gas burners and electric heaters were invented. The tin was partly changed to white powder, and the water level rose in the jar until only four-fifths as much air was left as there had been at the start. Further heating caused no detectable change. In another experiment Lavoisier heated tin in a sealed flask until as much as possible was converted to powder. The flask was weighed accurately before and after heating, and the two weights proved to be identical. Then the flask was opened, and air rushed in. With the additional air, the weight of the flask was greater than it had been at the start—and by the same amount as the increase in weight of the tin.

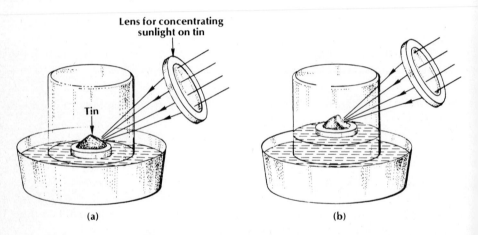

Fig. 3-2 Lavoisier's experiment showing that tin upon heating combines with a gas from the air: (a) Before heating; (b) after heating. The tin is partly changed to a white powder, and the water level rises until only four-fifths as much air is left as there was at the start. Further heating causes no additional change.

6. Arrange the steps of Lavoisier's second experiment in the order of their occurrence. You may refer to the passage as often as you wish.

_____ He weighed the flask accurately after heating, and the two weights proved identical.

_____ When the flask was opened, air rushed in.

_____ He heated tin in a sealed flask until as much as possible was converted to powder.

_____ With the additional air, the weight of the flask was greater than it had been at the start—and by the same amount as the increase in the weight of tin.

_____ He weighed the flask accurately before heating.

Answers: 3, 4, 2, 5, 1.

7. Although the author does not specifically state the conclusions drawn from these two experiments, we can conclude that the powder weighed more than the tin because:

a. The powder combined with certain elements in the water.

b. Heating metals always produces a weight change.

c. The tin, when heated, combines with a gas from the air.

Answer: c.

ELECTRIC CHARGES

Let us examine the behavior of electric charges more carefully. We begin by suspending a small pith ball from a silk thread, to serve as an indicator of charges in its vicinity. If touched with a rubber rod that has been stroked with fur, the pith ball jerks violently away and, thereafter, is strongly repelled whenever the rod is brought near (Fig. 3-3). We assume that the pith ball had no electric charge at the beginning of the experiment; at the instant of contact with the rod the ball acquired some of the charge on the rod and in this charged condition is repelled by the rod.

Now bring near the same pith ball a glass rod that has been rubbed with silk. The ball is no longer repelled but strongly attracted (Fig. 3-3). With the ball in this condition, therefore, the charge of the rubber rod repels it, and the glass rod attracts it. Now try the experiment in reverse: charge a second pith ball by touching it with the glass rod. It bounds away, evidently repelled. But the charged rubber rod attracts this second ball strongly.

We can draw only one conclusion: the charges on the two rods are somehow different. Furthermore, the kind of charge on one rod attracts the kind of the other, but each rod repels an object that has some of its own kind of charge. More simply, *like charges repel each other, unlike charges attract each other.*

Comprehensive experiments show that all electric charges that can be produced fall into one or the other of the two types described above; that is, they behave as though they originated on a rubber rod rubbed with fur or else on a glass rod rubbed with silk, regardless of their actual origin. Benjamin Franklin suggested names for these two basic kinds of electricity. He called the charge produced on a rubber rod rubbed with fur *negative charge*, the charge produced on a glass rod rubbed with silk *positive charge*. These definitions are the ones we follow today.

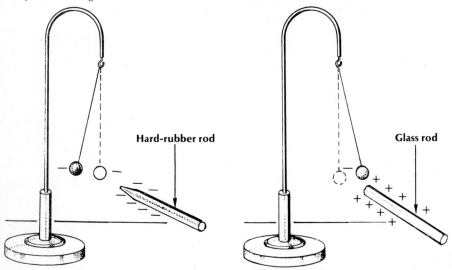

Hard-rubber rod   **Glass rod**

Fig. 3-3 A pith ball touched by a rubber rod that has been stroked with cat fur is repelled by the rod. When a glass rod that has been stroked with silk cloth is brought near, however, the pith ball is attracted to it. Performing the experiment in the reverse order has the same effect; hence the conclusion is that like charges repel each other, unlike charges attract each other.

Read the accompanying passage, and then answer the questions below. You may refer to the passage as often as you like.

1. What is the purpose of the experiment?

_____

_____

Answer (your own words): To examine different kinds of electrical charges.

2. What are the three objects used in the experiment?

a. _____

    as an indicator of charges.

b. _____

    to represent negative charges.

c. _____

    to represent positive charges.

Answer: a. A pith ball suspended from a silk thread
         b. A rubber rod rubbed with fur
         c. A glass rod rubbed with silk

3. Arrange these steps of the experiment in the order of their occurrence.

_____ The pith ball jerks violently away from the rubber rod.
_____ The pith ball is touched by the rubber rod.
_____ The pith ball is strongly attracted to the glass rod.
_____ The pith ball is touched with the glass rod.

Answers: 2, 1, 4, 3.

ELECTRIC CHARGES

Let us examine the behavior of electric charges more carefully. We begin by suspending a small pith ball from a silk thread, to serve as an indicator of charges in its vicinity. If touched with a rubber rod that has been stroked with fur, the pith ball jerks violently away and, thereafter, is strongly repelled whenever the rod is brought near (Fig. 3-3). We assume that the pith ball had no electric charge at the beginning of the experiment; at the instant of contact with the rod the ball acquired some of the charge on the rod and in this charged condition is repelled by the rod.

Now bring near the same pith ball a glass rod that has been rubbed with silk. The ball is no longer repelled but strongly attracted (Fig. 3-3). With the ball in this condition, therefore, the charge of the rubber rod repels it, and the glass rod attracts it. Now try the experiment in reverse: charge a second pith ball by touching it with the glass rod. It bounds away, evidently repelled. But the charged rubber rod attracts this second ball strongly.

We can draw only one conclusion: the charges on the two rods are somehow different. Furthermore, the kind of charge on one rod attracts the kind of the other, but each rod repels an object that has some of its own kind of charge. More simply, *like charges repel each other, unlike charges attract each other.*

Comprehensive experiments show that all electric charges that can be produced fall into one or the other of the two types described above; that is, they behave as though they originated on a rubber rod rubbed with fur or else on a glass rod rubbed with silk, regardless of their actual origin. Benjamin Franklin suggested names for these two basic kinds of electricity. He called the charge produced on a rubber rod rubbed with fur *negative charge*, the charge produced on a glass rod rubbed with silk *positive charge*. These definitions are the ones we follow today.

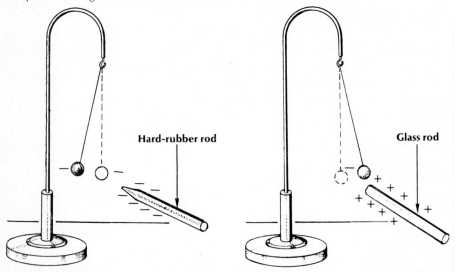

Hard-rubber rod

Glass rod

Fig. 3-3 A pith ball touched by a rubber rod that has been stroked with cat fur is repelled by the rod. When a glass rod that has been stroked with silk cloth is brought near, however, the pith ball is attracted to it. Performing the experiment in the reverse order has the same effect; hence the conclusion is that like charges repel each other, unlike charges attract each other.

4. Now, the author explains, we try the experiment in reverse. Arrange these steps of the reverse experiment (as described in the passage) in the order of their occurrence.

_____ The pith ball is touched by a glass rod.
_____ The pith ball is attracted to the rubber rod.
_____ The pith ball is repelled by the glass rod.
_____ The pith ball is touched with the rubber rod.

Answers: 1, 4, 2, 3.

5. We can see from the above that:
    a. The pith ball is always positively charged.
    b. The pith ball assumes the charge of whichever rod it is first touched with.
    c. The pith ball is always repelled by the glass rod.
    d. The pith ball assumes the opposite charge from that of the rod it is first touched with.

Answer: b.

6. The author concludes that:
    a. There are negative and positive charges.
    b. Pith balls are electrically neutral.
    c. Like charges repel each other; unlike charges attract each other.
    d. Like charges attract each other; unlike charges repel each other.

Answer: c.

TASTE DISCRIMINATION

Obtain four applicator sticks and roll a small swab of absorbent cotton around one end of each. Rinse your mouth with water. Dip one of the applicators into a 5% sucrose solution, and then touch the following regions of your tongue with the sucrose-moistened cotton: tip, front side edge, upper front center, upper back center, back side edge, lower center.

Record where a sweet sensation is most distinct, less distinct, or not registered at all. Rinse your mouth.

Using separate applicators, repeat the above test with each of the following solutions, in the order given: 10% NaCl, 1% acetic acid, 0.001% quinine. Rinse your mouth thoroughly after each series of tests. Record as above for salty, sour, and bitter sensations. *Tabulate* all data and interpret.

Read the accompanying passage, and then answer the questions below. You may refer to the passage as often as you like.

1. What four solutions are used in the experiment?

_____

_____

_____

_____

Answers: 5% sucrose solution
           10% NaCl
           1% acetic acid
           0.001% quinine

2. Arrange the following steps of the experiment in the order of their occurrence.
   _____ Dip one of the applicators into the 5% sucrose solution.
   _____ Rinse your mouth with water.
   _____ Roll a small swab of absorbent cotton around one end of each of four applicator sticks.
   _____ Record where a sweet sensation is most distinct, less distinct, or not registered at all.
   _____ Touch the following regions of your tongue with the sucrose-moistened cotton: tip, front side edge, upper front center, upper back center, back side edge, lower center.
   _____ Repeat the test with the other three solutions.

Answers: 3, 2, 1, 5, 4, 6.

TASTE DISCRIMINATION

Obtain four applicator sticks and roll a small swab of absorbent cotton around one end of each. Rinse your mouth with water. Dip one of the applicators into a 5% sucrose solution, and then touch the following regions of your tongue with the sucrose-moistened cotton: tip, front side edge, upper front center, upper back center, back side edge, lower center.

Record where a sweet sensation is most distinct, less distinct, or not registered at all. Rinse your mouth.

Using separate applicators, repeat the above test with each of the following solutions, in the order given: 10% NaCl, 1% acetic acid, 0.001% quinine. Rinse your mouth thoroughly after each series of tests. Record as above for salty, sour, and bitter sensations. *Tabulate* all data and interpret.

3. Considering the steps taken, what do you think is the purpose of this experiment?

_____

_____

Answer (your own words): To determine which parts of the tongue are used for discriminating different types of tastes.

ARCHIMEDES' PRINCIPLE

It is a matter of common experience that bodies are apparently lighter under water than in air. A fresh egg sinks in pure water, but floats in salty water. A piece of iron sinks in water, but floats in mercury. If a diver picks up a stone under water and brings it to the surface, he finds that the stone is much heavier above the surface. The principle which explains these observations, discovered by the distinguished Greek mathematician and physicist Archimedes, states that:

A body immersed in a fluid is buoyed up by a force equal to the weight of the fluid displaced.

An experimental verification of Archimedes' principle can be obtained by use of the equipment of Fig. 3-4. A hollow cylindrical cup and a piece of brass turned so that it will just fill the cavity inside the cup are suspended from one arm of a balance, and the weights necessary to restore equilibrium are added to the other pan. When a vessel of water is brought up in such a way that the cylinder C is completely submerged, the side of the balance carrying the cylinder rises, showing that the water is pushing upward on the cylinder. If water is now poured into the cup until it is full, the original equilibrium of the balance is restored. The cylinder is buoyed up by a force equal to the weight of the water displaced.

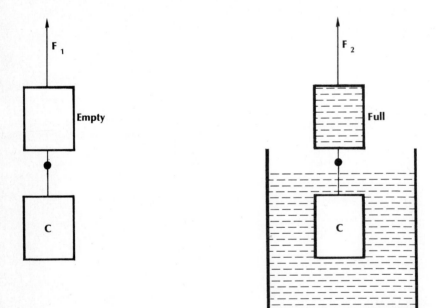

Fig. 3-4 How cylinder C is buoyed up by a force equal to the weight of the fluid it displaces is shown in this experiment. F_1 equals F_2 when displaced liquid is transferred to container above.

Read the accompanying passage, and then answer the questions below. You may refer to the passage as often as necessary.

1. The Greek mathematician and physicist Archimedes discovered the principle of _____

Answer: buoyant force.

2. Arrange these steps of the experiment which verifies Archimedes' principle in the order of their occurrence.

_____ If water is poured into the cup until it is full, the original equilibrium of balance is restored.

_____ A vessel of water is brought up in such a way that the cylinder is completely submerged.

_____ A hollow cylindrical cup and a piece of brass turned so that it will just fill the cavity inside the cup are suspended from one arm of a balance, and the weights necessary to restore equilibrium are added to the other pan.

_____ The side of the balance carrying the cylinder rises.

Answers: 4, 2, 1, 3.

3. This experiment supports Archimedes' principle because the cylinder is buoyed up by:

_____

Answer (your own words): a force equal to the weight of the water displaced.

BUOYANT EFFECT OF AIR

Archimedes' principle applies to all fluids. In general, the densities of gases are much smaller than those of liquids, and the buoyant effects are correspondingly reduced. Nevertheless there are many examples of situations in which the buoyant effects of gases—in particular of air—are of considerable importance. The density of air is 1.293 kg/m³ at 0°C and one standard atmosphere pressure.

A simple demonstration of the buoyant effect of air may be made by suspending a lead ball (Fig. 3-5) from one side of a small balance and a large hollow brass sphere from the other side. The hollow sphere is just heavy enough to balance the lead ball when both are in air. If the balance, together with the suspended spheres, is placed under a bell jar and nearly all the air removed by means of a pump, the lead ball no longer balances the hollow sphere. This is because the buoyancy of the air on the hollow brass sphere is greater than on the lead ball; when this lift has been removed, the true weights of the spheres become evident, and the hollow sphere weighs more than the lead sphere.

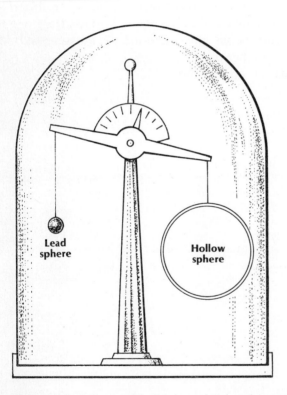

Lead sphere

Hollow sphere

Fig. 3-5 A body immersed in air is buoyed up by a force equal to the weight of the air it displaces. The two spheres balance one another at normal air pressure, but when air is evacuated from the jar, the larger sphere sinks.

Read the accompanying passage, and then answer the questions below. You may refer to the passage if necessary.

1. The purpose of this experiment is to demonstrate the buoyant effect of _____

Answer: air.

2. Arrange the steps of the experiment in the order of their occurrence.
_____ The balance is placed under a bell jar.
_____ A lead ball is suspended from one side of a balance and a large hollow sphere from the other.
_____ The lead ball no longer balances the hollow sphere; the sphere weighs more.
_____ Nearly all the air is removed by means of a pump.

Answers: 2, 1, 4, 3.

3. We can conclude that:
   a. The buoyant force of air on the lead ball made it appear to be of the same weight as the hollow sphere.
   b. Removing the air from the bell jar allows us to see buoyancy at work.
   c. The buoyant force of air is greater on the hollow sphere and makes it appear to be as light as the lead ball.
   d. The hollow sphere actually weighs less than the lead ball.

Answer: c.

Part 4
Graphic Aids

Because of the technical nature of scientific material, it is often difficult to understand complex descriptions. Graphic representations can help by summarizing and unifying information in such a way that the reader is able to see at a glance relationships that would otherwise require considerable explanation.

In this section we will study three kinds of graphic aids: graphs, tables, and diagrams from both the physical sciences and the social sciences.

A TYPICAL GRAPH

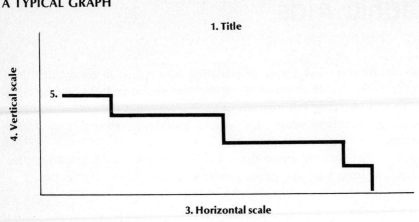

GRAPHS

A graph is a special type of diagram which usually presents a group of interrelated facts by means of points placed at certain distances from two intersecting lines called axes. The points may be connected (line graphs) or supported by columns (bar graphs).

A graph usually has:

1. A *title* which explains generally what kind of material the graph contains. You should always read the title carefully.
2. A *caption* or description which further explains the material.
3. A *horizontal scale*.
4. A *vertical scale*.
5. Some indication of the relationship between the horizontal scale and the vertical scale: a line or lines, a curve, a visible pattern of ups and downs (such as in a bar graph), etc.

Of course graphs differ. For variety, graphs are also presented as circles (circular graphs) or as figures of different sizes (pictographs), but these are useful only where great precision is not necessary.

**LEARNING IS USUALLY FASTER UNDER
CONDITIONS OF DISTRIBUTED PRACTICE**

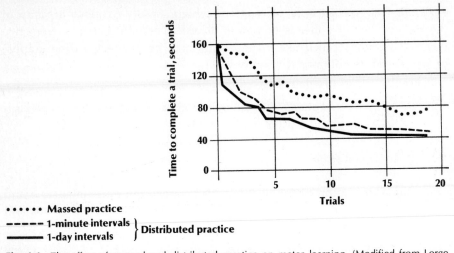

• • • • • **Massed practice**

‒ ‒ ‒ ‒ ‒ **1-minute intervals** ⎱
──── **1-day intervals** ⎰ **Distributed practice**

Fig. 4-1   The effect of massed and distributed practice on motor learning. (Modified from Lorge, 1930.)

Read the accompanying graph, and then answer the questions below. You may refer to the graph as often as you wish.

1. The title of this graph is:

_____

Answer: Learning Is Usually Faster under Conditions of Distributed Practice

2. The vertical scale represents _____; the horizontal scale represents _____

Answer: time to complete a trial, seconds; number of trials.

3. At fifteen trials, how long did it take a person experiencing massed practice to complete the trial? _____

Answer: Eighty seconds.

4. At fifteen trials, how much difference was there between the massed practice and the distributed practice (1-day) subjects? _____

Answer: About forty seconds.

5. The 1-minute interval distributed practice line is more like which line?

Answer: The 1-day interval line.

6. What general conclusion is drawn from the data presented?

_____

_____

Answer: Learning is usually faster under conditions of distributed practice.

**MOST PATIENTS ADMITTED FOR THE FIRST TIME TO MENTAL
HOSPITALS HAVE BRAIN SYNDROMES OR PSYCHOTIC DISORDERS**

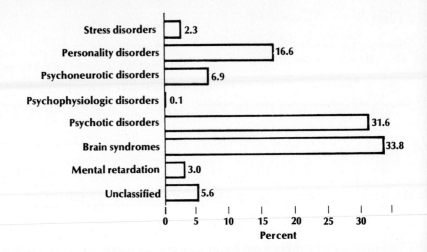

Fig. 4-2 Percentages of patients in particular diagnostic categories upon first admission to public mental hospitals. (From Kisker, 1964. Adapted from data furnished by the National Institute of Mental Health, 1963.)

Study the accompanying graph, and then answer the questions below. You may refer to the graph as often as you like.

1. What is the title of the graph?

_____

_____

Answer: Most Patients Admitted for the First Time to Mental Hospitals Have Brain Syndromes or Psychotic Disorders

2. The vertical scale lists _____; the horizontal scale represents _____

Answer: kinds of disorders; percent of occurrence of disorders.

3. What two types of disorder are found most frequently among patients first admitted to public mental hospitals? _____ and _____

Answer: Brain syndromes and psychotic disorders.

4. What type of disorder occurred least frequently among patients first admitted to public mental hospitals? _____

Answer: Psychophysiologic.

5. What percent of the patients had personality disorders? _____

Answer: 16.6 percent.

6. What is the *total* percent of patients with brain syndromes and patients with psychotic disorders in this study? _____

Answer: 65.4 percent.

THE GOVERNMENT DOLLAR (FISCAL YEAR 1965 ESTIMATE)

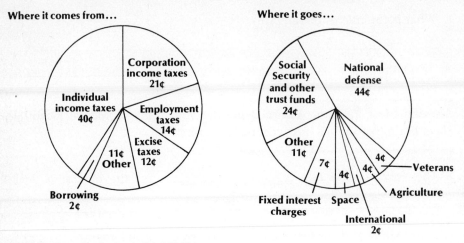

Fig. 4-3   (From *The Budget in Brief,* 1965.)

Study the accompanying graph, and then answer the questions below. You may refer to the graph as often as you wish.

1. What two things does this graph represent?

a. _____

b. _____

Answer: a.   Where the government dollar comes from.
          b.   Where it goes.

2. What fiscal year is represented by the graph? _____

Answer: 1965.

3. Where does most of the government's money come from? _____
   _____

Answer: Individual income taxes.

4. Where is most of the government's money spent? _____

Answer: National defense.

5. Government spending for education must be less than _____ of every dollar because it is included in the segment labeled _____

Answer: 11 cents, other.

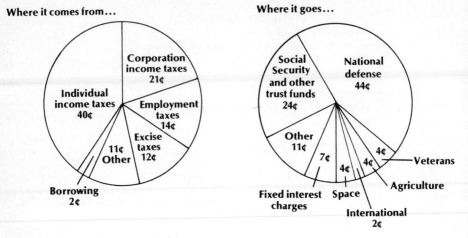

THE GOVERNMENT DOLLAR (FISCAL YEAR 1965 ESTIMATE)

Fig. 4-3   (From *The Budget in Brief*, 1965.)

6. How much of every dollar comes from various taxes? _____

Answer: 87 cents.

7. National defense and space take how much of every dollar? _____

Answer: 48 cents.

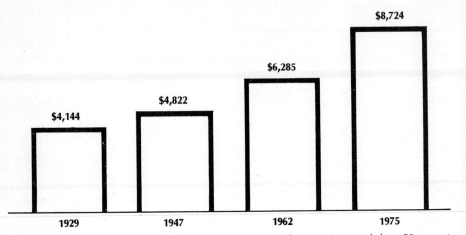

AVERAGE INCOME PER FAMILY AFTER TAXES (IN 1960 DOLLARS)

Fig. 4-4   In 33 years—1929 to 1962—average family income after taxes increased about 50 percent. It will rise another 40 percent by 1975. (From *Newsletter,* Twentieth Century Fund, Spring, 1964.)

Study the accompanying graph, and then answer the questions below. You may refer to the graph as often as you want.

1. The title of this graph is:

_____

Answer: Average Income per Family after Taxes (in 1960 Dollars)

_____

2. The vertical scale indicates _____

Answer: amount of income.

_____

3. The horizontal scale represents _____

Answer: years.

_____

4. The graph shows the relationship between _____

   and _____

Answer: amount of income and years.

_____

5. In what year was the average income per family $6,285? _____.

Answer: 1962.

_____

6. What was the average income per family in 1929? _____

Answer: $4,144.

_____

A TYPICAL TABLE

1. TITLE

2. List of items		3. List of statistics	

GRAPHIC AIDS 171

TABLES

When a writer wishes to make a large amount of information easily available, he condenses his facts and arranges them into a collection called a table. A table usually has:

1. A *title*. As with graphs, you should read the title carefully because it will tell you what the table is about.
2. A *list of items*. This list will usually have a title above it.
3. A list (or lists) of *statistics* giving information about the first list of items.

All tables will not conform exactly to this pattern, but they will usually contain the three parts listed above.

TABLE 4-1   MEDIAN MONEY INCOME OF MALE PERSONS WITH INCOME,
BY OCCUPATION GROUP, 1950 AND 1962

Occupational Group	1950	1962	% Increase
Professional, technical, and kindred workers....................	$4,073	$7,310	79%
Farmers and farm managers..........	1,496	2,351	57%
Managers, officials and proprietors, except farm	3,814	6,821	79%
Clerical and kindred workers........	3,103	5,331	72%
Sales workers	3,137	5,369	71%
Craftsmen, foremen, and kindred workers.....................	3,293	5,871	78%
Operatives and kindred workers	2,790	4,832	73%
Service workers, except private household	2,303	3,684	60%
Farm laborers and foremen	854	1,353	58%
Laborers, except farm and mine......	1,909	3,202	68%
All employed male civilians.........	2,831	5,240	85%

SOURCE: *Statistical Abstract of the United States,* 1964, p. 343.

Study the accompanying table, and then answer the questions below. You may refer to the table as often as you like.

1. What is the title of this table?

_____

_____

Answer: Median Money Income of Male Persons with Income, by Occupation Group, 1950 and 1962.

2. What was the income of "professional, technical, and kindred workers" in 1950? _____

Answer: $4,073.

3. What was the income of the same group in 1962? _____

Answer: $7,310.

4. What was the percent increase for this group between 1950 and 1962?

Answer: 79 percent.

5. Which individual group showed the lowest percent increase in income between 1950 and 1962? _____

Answer: Farmers and farm managers.

**TABLE 4-1 MEDIAN MONEY INCOME OF MALE PERSONS WITH INCOME,
BY OCCUPATION GROUP, 1950 AND 1962**

Occupational Group	1950	1962	% Increase
Professional, technical, and kindred workers...................	$4,073	$7,310	79%
Farmers and farm managers.........	1,496	2,351	57%
Managers, officials and proprietors, except farm..................	3,814	6,821	79%
Clerical and kindred workers........	3,103	5,331	72%
Sales workers...................	3,137	5,369	71%
Craftsmen, foremen, and kindred workers.....................	3,293	5,871	78%
Operatives and kindred workers.....	2,790	4,832	73%
Service workers, except private household......................	2,303	3,684	60%
Farm laborers and foremen.........	854	1,353	58%
Laborers, except farm and mine......	1,909	3,202	68%
All employed male civilians.........	2,831	5,240	85%

SOURCE: *Statistical Abstract of the United States,* 1964, p. 343.

6. Which two groups showed the highest percent increase in income during this same period? _____ ;

_____

Answer: Professional, technical, and kindred workers; managers, officials and proprietors, except farm.

7. What was the percent of increase of income for all male workers during the period? _____

Answer: 85 percent.

TABLE 4-2   BODILY SYMPTOMS OF FEAR IN COMBAT FLYING
Over 4,000 fliers in World War II were asked how often
they experienced different symptoms in combat flying.

	Percentage Answering		
Symptom	"Often"	"Some-times"	Total
Pounding heart and rapid pulse	30	56	86
Muscles very tense	30	53	83
Easily irritated, angry, or "sore"	22	58	80
Dryness of the throat or mouth	30	50	80
"Nervous perspiration" or "cold sweat"	26	53	79
"Butterflies" in the stomach	23	53	76
Sense of unreality, that this couldn't be happening	20	49	69
Need to urinate very frequently	25	40	65
Trembling	11	53	64
Confused or rattled	3	50	53
Weak or faint	4	37	41
After mission, not being able to remember details of what happened	5	34	39
Sick to the stomach	5	33	38
Not being able to concentrate	3	32	35

SOURCE: Adopted from Laurance F. Shaffer, "Fear and Courage in Aerial Combat," *Journal of Consulting Psychology,* vol. XI, no. 3, 1947, p. 139.

Study the accompanying table, and then answer the questions below. You may refer to the table as often as you wish.

1. This table shows the frequency of _____ in combat flying.

Answer: bodily symptoms of fear

2. Which three symptoms occurred "often" most frequently?

   a. _____

   b. _____

   c. _____

Answers: *a.* Pounding heart and rapid pulse.
         b. Muscles very tense.
         c. Dryness of throat or mouth.

3. Which single symptom was present most frequently (both "often" *and* "sometimes") for all pilots? _____

Answer: Pounding heart and rapid pulse.

4. What percentage of pilots "often" experienced trembling? _____

Answer: 11 percent.

TABLE 4-2   BODILY SYMPTOMS OF FEAR IN COMBAT FLYING
Over 4,000 fliers in World War II were asked how often
they experienced different symptoms in combat flying.

Symptom	"Often"	"Some-times"	Total
		Percentage Answering	
Pounding heart and rapid pulse	30	56	86
Muscles very tense	30	53	83
Easily irritated, angry, or "sore"	22	58	80
Dryness of the throat or mouth	30	50	80
"Nervous perspiration" or "cold sweat"	26	53	79
"Butterflies" in the stomach	23	53	76
Sense of unreality, that this couldn't be happening	20	49	69
Need to urinate very frequently	25	40	65
Trembling	11	53	64
Confused or rattled	3	50	53
Weak or faint	4	37	41
After mission, not being able to remember details of what happened	5	34	39
Sick to the stomach	5	33	38
Not being able to concentrate	3	32	35

SOURCE: Adopted from Laurance F. Shaffer, "Fear and Courage in Aerial Combat," *Journal of Consulting Psychology,* vol. XI, no. 3, 1947, p. 139.

5. What percentage of pilots "sometimes" experienced "butterflies" in the stomach? ═══════════

Answer: 53 percent.

6. What was the total percentage of pilots who experienced "weak or faint" feelings (both "sometimes" and "often")? ═══════════

Answer: 41 percent.

TABLE 4-3   BEAUFORT SCALE OF WIND FORCE

Beaufort number	Name	Characteristics	Velocity, miles per hour
0	Calm	Smoke rises vertically	Less than 1
1	Light air	Smoke drifts	1–3
2	Slight breeze	Leaves rustle	4–7
3	Gentle breeze	Leaves and twigs move constantly	8–12
4	Moderate breeze	Raises dust and small branches move	13–18
5	Fresh breeze	Small trees sway	19–24
6	Strong breeze	Large branches move	25–31
7	Moderate gale	Whole trees in motion	32–38
8	Fresh gale	Tree twigs are broken	39–46
9	Strong gale	Some damage occurs	47–54
10	Whole gale	Trees uprooted and limbs broken	55–63
11	Storm	Widespread damage	64–75
12	Hurricane	Great damage	Above 75

Study the accompanying table, and then answer the questions below. You may refer to the table as often as you like.

1. What is the title of the table?

_____

Answer: Beaufort Scale of Wind Force

2. What are the characteristics of a fresh breeze according to the table?

Answer: Small trees sway.

3. What is the velocity (miles per hour) of a fresh breeze? _____

Answer: 19–24 miles per hour.

4. What is the Beaufort number for a hurricane? _____

Answer: 12.

5. A wind velocity of 13–18 miles per hour would have a Beaufort rank of _____

Answer: 4.

6. What would we call a wind classified as 3 on the scale? _____

Answer: Gentle breeze.

TABLE 4-3   BEAUFORT SCALE OF WIND FORCE

Beaufort number	Name	Characteristics	Velocity, miles per hour
0	Calm	Smoke rises vertically	Less than 1
1	Light air	Smoke drifts	1–3
2	Slight breeze	Leaves rustle	4–7
3	Gentle breeze	Leaves and twigs move constantly	8–12
4	Moderate breeze	Raises dust and small branches move	13–18
5	Fresh breeze	Small trees sway	19–24
6	Strong breeze	Large branches move	25–31
7	Moderate gale	Whole trees in motion	32–38
8	Fresh gale	Tree twigs are broken	39–46
9	Strong gale	Some damage occurs	47–54
10	Whole gale	Trees uprooted and limbs broken	55–63
11	Storm	Widespread damage	64–75
12	Hurricane	Great damage	Above 75

7. What characteristics could we expect to see happen if a wind were classified as 10 on the scale? _____

Answer: Uprooted trees and broken limbs.

8. How fast does the wind have to blow to be classified as a storm? _____

Answer: 64–75 miles per hour.

9. What does the table tell us about a fresh gale?
   a. Beaufort rank: _____
   b. Characteristics: _____
   c. Velocity: _____

Answers: a. 8.
          b. Tree twigs are broken.
          c. 39–46 miles per hour.

A TYPICAL DIAGRAM
1. Title

> **2. Illustration**
>
> **3. Words describing the illustration**

4. Caption or description

DIAGRAMS

A diagram is a simplified drawing used to show relationships, processes, or functions. Diagrams are very useful in science to represent things which are difficult to visualize or imagine. A diagram usually has:

1. A *title*. Again, as with graphs and tables, the first step in understanding a diagram is to read the title carefully.
2. An *illustration* (the diagram itself).
3. Words or numbers of letters on the illustration which help to describe it.
4. A *caption* or description of the illustration.

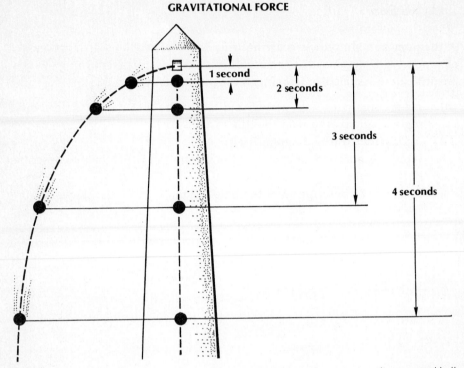

Fig. 4-5   When one ball is thrown horizontally from a building at the same time that a second ball is dropped vertically, the two reach the ground simultaneously because both have the same downward acceleration.

Study the accompanying diagram, and then answer the questions below. You may refer to the diagram as often as you like.

1. What is the title of this diagram?

_____

Answer: Gravitational Force

2. What is the difference between the two falling balls?

_____

Answer: One is thrown horizontally; the other is dropped vertically.

3. After two seconds, which ball has fallen farther?

_____

Answer: Neither—they have both fallen the same distance.

4. After four seconds, which ball has fallen farther?

_____

Answer: Neither—they have both fallen the same distance.

5. We can conclude that bodies fall with the same _____

Answer: downward acceleration.

WHEN THE EYEBALL IS TOO SHORT, A PERSON IS FARSIGHTED; WHEN IT IS TOO LONG, HE IS NEARSIGHTED

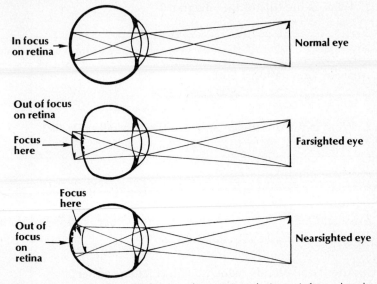

Fig. 4-6   Farsightedness and nearsightedness. In the normal person (top) the image is focused on the retina. The farsighted person (middle) has an eyeball that is too short and focuses images on a plane behind the retina. The nearsighted person (bottom) has an eyeball that is too long and focuses images on a plane in front of the retina. (Modified from Ruch, 1958.)

Study the accompanying diagram, and then answer the questions below. You may refer to the diagram as often as necessary.

1. The title of this diagram is:

_____

_____

Answer: When the Eyeball Is Too Short, a Person Is Farsighted; When It Is Too Long, He Is Nearsighted

2. What determines whether an eye is classified normal, farsighted, or near-sighted? _____

Answer: Length (shape) of eyeball.

3. When an eye is normal, where does the image focus? _____

Answer: On the retina.

4. In farsightedness the image focuses _____

Answer: beyond the retina.

5. In a nearsighted eye, the image is focused _____

Answer: in a plane in front of the retina.

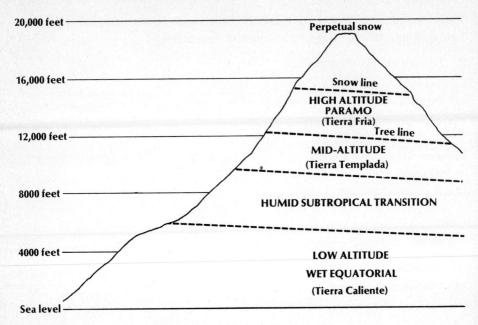

Fig. 4-7   The zoning of mountain climates in the central Andes.

Study the accompanying diagram, and then answer the questions below. You may refer to the diagram as often as you like.

1. What does this diagram represent?

_____

Answer: Zoning of mountain climates in the central Andes.

2. How many climate zones are indicated by the diagram? _____

Answer: Five.

3. At about what altitude is the tree line in the Andes? _____

Answer: 12,000 feet.

4. The wet equatorial climate tapers off at about _____ feet.

Answer: 5,000

5. What is the chief characteristic of the altitude above 16,000 feet? _____

Answer: Perpetual snow.

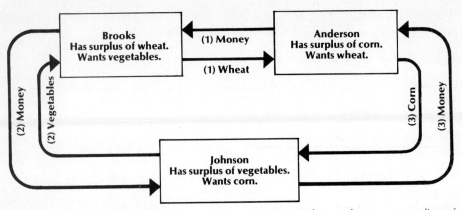

Fig. 4-8 *Money facilitates trade where wants do not coincide.* By the use of money as a medium of exchange, trade can be accomplished, as indicated by the arrows, despite a non-coincidence of wants. By facilitating exchange, the use of money permits an economy to realize the efficiencies of specialization.

Study the accompanying diagram, and then answer the questions below. You may refer to the diagram as often as you like.

1. What is the purpose of the figure?

_____

Answer: To show how money facilitates trade where wants do not coincide.

2. What three commodities are involved in the trading? _____

Answer: Wheat, corn, and vegetables.

3. The exchange of commodities is represented by the (inner, outer) set of arrows.

Answer: inner

4. Since Brooks wants vegetables, he will have to deal with _____

Answer: Johnson.

5. Why can't Brooks trade his wheat for Johnson's vegetables?

_____

Answer: Because Johnson wants corn.

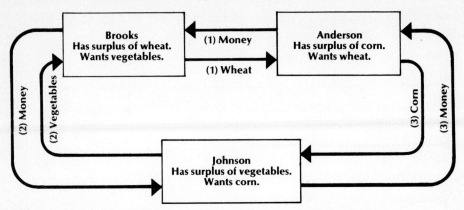

Fig. 4-8 *Money facilitates trade where wants do not coincide.* By the use of money as a medium of exchange, trade can be accomplished, as indicated by the arrows, despite a non-coincidence of wants. By facilitating exchange, the use of money permits an economy to realize the efficiencies of specialization.

6. Without money, what will Brooks have to do to get Johnson's vegetables?

_____

_____

Answer: Trade his wheat for corn with Anderson, and then trade the corn with Johnson.

7. The diagram shows how money makes it easier for Brooks to get Johnson's vegetables. What do the arrows between Brooks and Anderson mean?

_____

Answer: Brooks gives Anderson wheat for money.

8. What do the arrows indicate happens between Brooks and Johnson?

_____

Answer: Brooks gives Johnson money for vegetables.

9. From having studied the diagram, we can see more clearly how _____

Answer: money facilitates trade.

Part 5
Understanding
Principles

In this final section of the book you will find passages taken from textbooks in the physical sciences. However, these passages are less technical than those we studied earlier. In these, *general* concepts of science are discussed.

Keeping in mind the previous work you have done (finding the principal idea, recognizing the details, understanding experiments and graphic aids), in these exercises you will choose from four statements the one which best summarizes what the passage is about. In a general sense, we are again finding the principal idea, but in passages which are less technical in their content.

CHANGING CELLS

No living unit is ever exactly like any other or exactly the same from moment to moment; living matter is not a static, passive material. In a cell, for example, new substances enter continuously, wastes and manufactured products leave continuously, and substances in the interior are continuously transformed chemically and redistributed physically. As a result, living matter is always in agitation. To the human observer a tree may appear to be a rather placid, inactive structure; but if the cell contents of the tree could be seen, they would all be noted to be in unceasing motion, interacting and changing. Consequently, the tree as a whole changes continuously, and so indeed does every kind of living material.

Read the passage carefully. Then choose the principal idea from the four statements below.

   a. While the living matter of human beings is in constant flux, that of trees and plants remains static.

   b. All living matter is interacting and changing at all times.

   c. Living matter varies from very static to very active states.

   d. The study of living matter can be very rewarding to the human observer.

Answer: *b.*

THE CELL THEORY

The generalization that all organisms consist entirely of cells and cell products is known as the *cell theory*. Formulated in 1838 by the German biologists Schleiden and Schwann, this theory rapidly became one of the fundamental cornerstones of modern biology and, with minor qualifications, it still has that status today. In 1831, the English biologist Robert Brown discovered the presence of nuclei within cells, and in 1839 the Bohemian biologist Purkinje coined the general term *protoplasm* for the living substance out of which cells are made. Virchow in 1855 concluded that *"omnis cellula e cellula"* —new living cells can arise only by reproduction of pre-existing living cells. This was an important recognition of the continuity of life, well in line with what was then already known about the growth and development of organisms and about evolution.

Read the passage carefully. Then choose the principal idea from the four statements below.

a. The once popular cell theory is no longer accepted as valid.
b. The mystery of cell reproduction was reconciled with the cell theory in 1838 by the German biologists Schleiden and Brown.
c. The theory of evolution had its beginnings in the cell theory.
d. The cell theory is still considered a fundamental cornerstone of modern biology.

Answer: *d.*

LIMITATIONS OF SCIENCE

First, scientific investigation defines the domain of science. Anything that is amenable to scientific investigation, now or in the future, is or will be within the domain of science; anything that is not amenable to such investigation is not within the scientific domain.

An awareness of these limits can help us to avoid many inappropriate controversies. For example, does the idea of God lend itself to scientific scrutiny? Suppose we wish to test the hypothesis that God is universal and exists everywhere and in everything. Being untested as yet, this hypothesis could be right or wrong. An experiment about God would then require experimental control, that is, two situations, one with God and one without, but otherwise identical.

If our hypothesis is correct, God would indeed exist everywhere. Hence He would be present in every test we could possibly make, and we would never be able to devise a situation in which God is not present. Yet we need such a situation for a controlled experiment. But if our hypothesis is wrong, He would not exist and would therefore be absent from any test we could possibly make. We would then never be able to devise a situation in which God *is* present. Yet we would need such a situation for a controlled experiment.

Right or wrong, our hypothesis is untestable, since we cannot run a controlled experiment. Therefore, we cannot carry out a scientific investigation. The point is that the concept of God falls outside the domain of science, and science cannot legitimately say anything about Him. It should be carefully noted that this is a far cry from saying "science disproves God," or "scientists must be godless; their method demands it." Nothing of the sort. Science specifically leaves anyone perfectly free to believe in any god whatsoever or in none. Many first-rate scientists are priests; many others are agnostics. Science commits you to nothing more, and to nothing less, than adherence to the ground rules of proper scientific inquiry.

The principal idea of the entire passage is:

   a. Since the hypothesis "God exists" is untested as yet, it could be right or wrong.

   b. It is difficult to construct a controlled experiment to test the hypothesis "God exists."

   c. The concept of God falls outside the domain of science and therefore the hypothesis "God exists" is untestable.

   d. Since the concept of God falls outside the domain of science, it follows that most scientists must be agnostics.

Answer: *c.*

THE ANIMAL KINGDOM

The world contains an enormous population of living animals, both kinds (more than 1,000,000) and numbers, and many others have lived during past geological time in the history of the earth. Animals differ in size, structure, internal physiological processes, manner of life, and other ways. The seas and lands, the lakes and streams, the swamps and meadows, the grasslands, the shrubs and trees of natural forests and cultivated places, the deserts, and all other types of environments each have distinctive kinds of animal inhabitants, some abundant and other rare. Most animals are affected by enemies, diseases, and competitors. The total of all these interactions comprises the "web of life" or the "balance of nature," a dynamic complex of forces, physical and biological, that affects every living organism.

All human beings, from primitive natives to the best educated, in country or city, are associated with some sorts of animal life. Certain kinds affect the well-being and health of mankind, for good or evil. The lives and habits of animals provide a highly interesting field of study for many people. There is already a great amount of detailed knowledge about animals—enough in book form to fill a large library—but much more is still to be learned, even about the most familiar animals.

The principal idea of this entire passage is:

a. The "web of life" or "balance of nature" is too complex for man to ever comprehend.

b. If animals were not affected by enemies, diseases, and competitors, they would overrun the earth.

c. All types of environments have distinctive kinds of animal inhabitants which can affect mankind for good or evil.

d. The total of interactions of animals with each other and with their environment is a dynamic complex of forces that affects every living organism.

Answer: *d.*

OBSERVATION, PROBLEM, HYPOTHESIS

Science generally begins with *observation*, the usual first step of scientific inquiry. At once this step puts a boundary around the scientific domain; something that cannot be observed cannot be investigated by science. Furthermore, for reasons that will become clear presently, it is necessary that an observation be *repeatable*, actually or potentially. One-time events are outside science (the one-time origin of the universe possibly excepted).

Correct observation is a most difficult art, acquired only after long experience and many errors. Everybody observes, with eyes, ears, touch, and all other senses, but few observe correctly. The problem here is largely unsuspected bias. People forever see what they *want* to see or what they think they *ought* to see. It is extremely hard to rid oneself of such unconscious prejudice and to see just what is actually there, no more and no less. Past experience, "common knowledge," and often teachers can be subtle obstacles to correct observation, and even experienced scientists may not always avoid them. That is why a scientific observation is not taken at face value until several scientists have repeated it independently and have reported the same thing. That is also a major reason why one-time, unrepeatable events generally cannot be investigated scientifically.

The principal idea under discussion in this passage is:

a. Because of unsuspected biases, scientific observations are not always accurate and must be repeated independently with the same results before they are accepted as valid.

b. The more experience one has, the better observer he will be.

c. Even scientists are unconsciously prejudiced.

d. If a scientific observation is proved true once, then the experiment need not be repeated.

Answer: a.

EXPERIMENTATION

Experimenting is the hardest part of the scientific process. There are no rules to follow; each experiment must be tackled in its own specific way.

The general nature of an experiment may be illustrated by the following example. Suppose that a chemical substance X has spilled accidentally into a culture dish full of certain disease-causing bacteria, and you observe that this chemical kills all the bacteria in the dish. Problem: can drug X be used to protect human beings against these disease-causing bacteria? Hypothesis: yes. Experiment: you find a patient with the particular bacterial disease and inject some of the drug into him. One possible result will be that the patient gets well fairly quickly, in which case you would conclude that your hypothesis is confirmed. Another possible result is that the patient remains ill or dies, and you would then conclude that your drug is worthless or dangerous.

However, in this example the so-called experiment was not really an experiment at all. First, no allowance was made for the possibility that different people might react differently to the same drug. Obviously, one would have to test the drug on many patients. Besides, one would make preliminary tests on mice or guinea pigs or monkeys. Second, the quantity of drug to be used was not determined. Clearly, a full range of dosages would have to be tested. Third, and most important, no account was taken of the possibility that your patient might have recovered (or died) even without your injecting the drug. What is needed here is *experimental control;* for every group of patients treated with the drug solution, a precisely equal group must be treated with a plain solution that does not contain the drug. Then, by comparing the control and the experimental groups, one can determine to what extent the results are actually attributable to the drug.

The principal idea of this entire passage is:

    a. Experimenting is the hardest part of the scientific process.

    b. One must be careful when experimenting with drugs because different people react differently.

    c. Without experimental control (using a control group and an experimental group), the results of experiments would be of dubious value.

    d. The results of experiments are always open to several interpretations.

Answer: *c.*

Conclusion
How to Use Your New Skills

You have now completed this program of instruction in improving scientific reading skills. Having been guided through a series of thought processes typical of those you will find in your science texts, you should now understand that science has its own characteristic way of arriving at knowledge. As a result, you are in a much better position to avoid confusing the things science deals with and the specialized equipment used in science with science itself. With your new skills, you should be able to avoid the mistake of attempting to memorize information and facts instead of learning how to observe and think in a specialized way.

In the future, as you read assignments in science texts, try to apply the things you have learned in this book. Determine the main point the author is making in each paragraph and then try to see how the details support his principal idea.

The study of science and the development of scientific attitudes represent another world of opportunity for any individual willing to undertake the self-discipline and dedication they require. If your understanding of scientific reading is made more meaningful for having studied this book, we both shall have been successful.

NOTES

NOTES

NOTES